When Someone You Love Has Dementia

Susan Elliot-Wright is a freelance writer and journalist specializing in health and parenting. Since training as a journalist while raising her two children, she has written hundreds of articles for newspapers and magazines, and is the author of four health information books for teenagers, as well as *Coping with Type 2 Diabetes* (2006), *Living with Heart Failure* (2006), *Overcoming Emotional Abuse* (2007), *Overcoming Insomnia* (2008) and *Coping with Epilepsy in Children and Young People* (2009), all published by Sheldon Press. She has a Master's degree in writing and has recently completed her first novel. She lives in Sheffield with her husband.

D1113219

Overcoming Common Problems Series

Selected titles

A full list of titles is available from Sheldon Press,
36 Causton Street, London SW1P 4ST and on our website at
www.sheldonpress.co.uk

The Assertiveness Handbook
Mary Hartley

Assertiveness: Step by step
Dr Windy Dryden and Daniel Constantinou

Backache: What you need to know
Dr David Delvin

Body Language: What you need to know
David Cohen

The Cancer Survivor's Handbook
Dr Terry Priestman

The Candida Diet Book
Karen Brody

The Chronic Fatigue Healing Diet
Christine Craggs-Hinton

The Chronic Pain Diet Book
Neville Shone

Cider Vinegar
Margaret Hills

The Complete Carer's Guide
Bridget McCall

The Confidence Book
Gordon Lamont

Confidence Works
Gladeana McMahon

Coping Successfully with Pain
Neville Shone

Coping Successfully with Panic Attacks
Shirley Trickett

Coping Successfully with Period Problems
Mary-Claire Mason

Coping Successfully with Psoriasis
Christine Craggs-Hinton

Coping Successfully with Ulcerative Colitis
Peter Cartwright

Coping Successfully with Varicose Veins
Christine Craggs-Hinton

Coping Successfully with Your Hiatus Hernia
Dr Tom Smith

Coping Successfully with Your Irritable Bowel
Rosemary Nicol

Coping When Your Child Has Cerebral Palsy
Jill Eckersley

Coping with Age-related Memory Loss
Dr Tom Smith

**Coping with Birth Trauma and Postnatal
Depression**
Lucy Jolin

Coping with Bowel Cancer
Dr Tom Smith

Coping with Candida
Shirley Trickett

Coping with Chemotherapy
Dr Terry Priestman

Coping with Chronic Fatigue
Trudie Chalder

Coping with Coeliac Disease
Karen Brody

Coping with Compulsive Eating
Ruth Searle

**Coping with Diabetes in Childhood and
Adolescence**
Dr Philippa Kaye

Coping with Diverticulitis
Peter Cartwright

Coping with Down's Syndrome
Fiona Marshall

Coping with Dyspraxia
Jill Eckersley

Coping with Eating Disorders and Body Image
Christine Craggs-Hinton

**Coping with Epilepsy in Children and Young
People**
Susan Elliot-Wright

Coping with Family Stress
Dr Peter Cheevers

Coping with Gout
Christine Craggs-Hinton

Coping with Hay Fever
Christine Craggs-Hinton

Coping with Headaches and Migraine
Alison Frith

Overcoming Common Problems Series

Coping with Hearing Loss
Christine Craggs-Hinton

Coping with Heartburn and Reflux
Dr Tom Smith

Coping with Kidney Disease
Dr Tom Smith

Coping with Life after Stroke
Dr Mareeni Raymond

Coping with Macular Degeneration
Dr Patricia Gilbert

Coping with a Mid-life Crisis
Derek Milne

Coping with PMS
Dr Farah Ahmed and Dr Emma Cordle

Coping with Polycystic Ovary Syndrome
Christine Craggs-Hinton

Coping with Postnatal Depression
Sandra L. Wheatley

Coping with Radiotherapy
Dr Terry Priestman

Coping with a Stressed Nervous System
Dr Kenneth Hambly and Alice Muir

Coping with Suicide
Maggie Helen

Coping with Tinnitus
Christine Craggs-Hinton

Coping with Type 2 Diabetes
Susan Elliot-Wright

Coping with Your Partner's Death: Your bereavement guide
Geoff Billings

The Depression Diet Book
Theresa Cheung

Depression: Healing emotional distress
Linda Hurcombe

Depressive Illness
Dr Tim Cantopher

Eating for a Healthy Heart
Robert Povey, Jacqui Morrell and Rachel Povey

Every Woman's Guide to Digestive Health
Jill Eckersley

The Fertility Handbook
Dr Philippa Kaye

The Fibromyalgia Healing Diet
Christine Craggs-Hinton

Free Your Life from Fear
Jenny Hare

Free Yourself from Depression
Colin and Margaret Sutherland

A Guide to Anger Management
Mary Hartley

Heal the Hurt: How to forgive and move on
Dr Ann Macaskill

Helping Children Cope with Anxiety
Jill Eckersley

Helping Children Cope with Grief
Rosemary Wells

How to Approach Death
Julia Tugendhat

How to be a Healthy Weight
Philippa Pigache

How to Beat Pain
Christine Craggs-Hinton

How to Cope with Difficult People
Alan Houel and Christian Godefroy

How to Fight Chronic Fatigue
Christine Craggs-Hinton

How to Get the Best from Your Doctor
Dr Tom Smith

How to Stop Worrying
Dr Frank Tallis

How to Talk to Your Child
Penny Oates

Hysterectomy: Is it right for you?
Janet Wright

The IBS Healing Plan
Theresa Cheung

Letting Go of Anxiety and Depression
Dr Windy Dryden

Living with Angina
Dr Tom Smith

Living with Asperger Syndrome
Dr Joan Gomez

Living with Autism
Fiona Marshall

Living with Bipolar Disorder
Dr Neel Burton

Living with Birthmarks and Blemishes
Gordon Lamont

Living with Crohn's Disease
Dr Joan Gomez

Living with Eczema
Jill Eckersley

Living with Fibromyalgia
Christine Craggs-Hinton

Living with Food Intolerance
Alex Gazzola

Overcoming Common Problems Series

Living with Gluten Intolerance
Jane Feinmann

Living with Grief
Dr Tony Lake

Living with Loss and Grief
Julia Tugendhat

Living with Osteoarthritis
Dr Patricia Gilbert

Living with Osteoporosis
Dr Joan Gomez

Living with Physical Disability and Amputation
Dr Keren Fisher

Living with Rheumatoid Arthritis
Philippa Pigache

Living with Schizophrenia
Dr Neel Burton and Dr Phil Davison

Living with a Seriously Ill Child
Dr Jan Aldridge

Living with Sjögren's Syndrome
Sue Dyson

Living with Type 1 Diabetes
Dr Tom Smith

Losing a Child
Linda Hurcombe

The Multiple Sclerosis Diet Book
Tessa Buckley

Osteoporosis: Prevent and treat
Dr Tom Smith

Overcome Your Fear of Flying
Professor Robert Bor, Dr Carina Eriksen and
Margaret Oakes

Overcoming Agoraphobia
Melissa Murphy

Overcoming Anorexia
Professor J. Hubert Lacey, Christine Craggs-Hinton
and Kate Robinson

Overcoming Anxiety
Dr Windy Dryden

Overcoming Back Pain
Dr Tom Smith

Overcoming Depression
Dr Windy Dryden and Sarah Opie

Overcoming Emotional Abuse
Susan Elliot-Wright

Overcoming Hurt
Dr Windy Dryden

Overcoming Insomnia
Susan Elliot-Wright

Overcoming Jealousy
Dr Windy Dryden

Overcoming Panic and Related Anxiety Disorders
Margaret Hawkins

Overcoming Procrastination
Dr Windy Dryden

Overcoming Shyness and Social Anxiety
Ruth Searle

Overcoming Tiredness and Exhaustion
Fiona Marshall

Reducing Your Risk of Cancer
Dr Terry Priestman

Safe Dieting for Teens
Lionda Ojeda

Self-discipline: How to get it and how to keep it
Dr Windy Dryden

The Self-Esteem Journal
Alison Waines

Simplify Your Life
Naomi Saunders

Sinusitis: Steps to healing
Dr Paul Carson

Stammering: Advice for all ages
Renée Byrne and Louise Wright

Stress-related Illness
Dr Tim Cantopher

Ten Steps to Positive Living
Dr Windy Dryden

Think Your Way to Happiness
Dr Windy Dryden and Jack Gordon

The Thinking Person's Guide to Happiness
Ruth Searle

Tranquillizers and Antidepressants: When to take them, how to stop
Professor Malcolm Lader

The Traveller's Good Health Guide
Dr Ted Lankester

Treating Arthritis Diet Book
Margaret Hills

Treating Arthritis: The drug-free way
Margaret Hills and Christine Horner

Treating Arthritis: More ways to a drug-free life
Margaret Hills

Understanding Obsessions and Compulsions
Dr Frank Tallis

When Someone You Love Has Dementia
Susan Elliot-Wright

When Someone You Love Has Depression
Barbara Baker

Overcoming Common Problems

When Someone You Love Has Dementia

SUSAN ELLIOT-WRIGHT

First published in Great Britain in 2010

Sheldon Press
36 Causton Street
London SW1P 4ST

Copyright © Susan Elliot-Wright 2010

The author and publisher have made every effort to ensure that the
external website and email addresses included in this book are correct and
up to date at the time of going to press. The author and publisher are not
responsible for the content, quality or continuing accessibility of the sites.

British Library Cataloguing-in-Publication Data
A catalogue record for this book is available from the British Library

ISBN 978–1–84709–075–1

1 3 5 7 9 10 8 6 4 2

Typeset by Fakenham Photosetting Ltd, Fakenham, Norfolk
Printed in Great Britain by Ashford Colour Press

Produced on paper from sustainable forests

Contents

Acknowledgements		viii
Introduction		ix
1	What is dementia?	1
2	Diagnosing dementia	10
3	After diagnosis	17
4	When the person with dementia is your partner	32
5	What treatments are available?	41
6	Coping with the practicalities – memory and behaviour	55
7	Coping with the practicalities – the physical side	67
8	Outside help, benefits and services	77
9	Permanent residential care	89
10	Coping with being a carer	96
Appendix: People you may encounter		106
Useful addresses		108
Further reading		113
Index		114

Acknowledgements

I would like to thank all those who were kind enough to share with me their experiences of dementia and their stories of how it has touched their lives. I would also like to thank Nicola at the Sheffield branch of the Alzheimer's Society for answering my many questions, and for providing a valuable insight into some of the problems experienced by people with dementia and their loved ones.

Introduction

We often use the term 'Alzheimer's' when what we actually mean is dementia. Although it's true that people with Alzheimer's do have dementia, people with dementia may not necessarily have Alzheimer's. Dementia is a gradual decline in certain brain functions, including memory, thinking and reasoning. It can be caused by a number of conditions or illnesses. Alzheimer's disease is the most common, and is thought to be the cause of over half of all dementia cases. Vascular dementia and Lewy body dementia each account for up to 20 per cent of cases, and less common causes make up the remainder. Around 6 per cent of people over 65 have dementia, with the illness becoming more common with increasing age and affecting one in three or four people over the age of 90. It is estimated that more than 700,000 people in the UK have dementia. Chapter 1 looks at the causes, symptoms and characteristics of the more common types.

According to an Alzheimer's Society report in 2007, there are around 595,000 unpaid carers of people with dementia in the UK. The carer may be a spouse or partner, a parent, a sibling or other relative or in-law, or it may be a friend or neighbour. Whether you will find yourself in the role of 'carer' or not, you are probably reading this book because someone close to you has been diagnosed with dementia, or because you're worried that he or she may be developing the condition.

The aim of the book is to help you to understand how the person might be affected by dementia, how this might impact on you and on the rest of the family, and how you can access as much practical help and support as you need.

Chapter 2 looks at how dementia is diagnosed, including ruling out other illnesses that may be causing the symptoms. This chapter also contains advice on getting medical help even if your loved one insists there's nothing wrong. Chapter 3 then looks at some of the feelings you might both experience if the diagnosis is indeed dementia, and Chapter 4 addresses some areas that may be of special concern if the person with dementia is your spouse or life partner. Drug treatments and non-drug therapies are covered in Chapter 5, which also looks at what can be done to help people with dementia to retain skills and abilities, and to stimulate their memory in enjoyable ways: for example, making a life-story book or putting together a memory box.

If you're living with and/or caring for someone with dementia, there will be all sorts of practical concerns as well as emotional ones, and there are sections to address a number of these issues, including advice on coping with memory loss (Chapter 6) and with continence problems (Chapter 7) and on finding out about and accessing other sources of help and support, such as claiming benefits and organizing respite care (Chapter 8) and arranging residential care (Chapter 9). The final chapter deals specifically with the topic of being a carer. The chapter looks at some of the emotions involved, some of the difficulties carers face and ways in which these may be overcome. It also includes a section on the very final stages of dementia, and how you might feel after your loved one has died.

Sadly, there is still a stigma attached to Alzheimer's disease and other dementias, and this means that dementia is rarely talked about. This situation is improving slightly, especially with the recent media attention attracted by well-known personalities speaking out about how dementia has touched their lives. Perhaps among the most popular is writer Sir Terry Pratchett, who has a rare form of Alzheimer's and has vowed to do all he can to raise awareness of the illness while he is able. In November 2008, as he presented a petition to the Prime Minister calling for more research funding, the author of the *Discworld* fantasy series said more open discussion was needed to break the superstition surrounding Alzheimer's. He made the observation that hardly a family in the land hasn't been affected in some way by dementia, and yet, as he says, 'because Alzheimer's affects the brain, we seem to have real difficulties about it'.

Stigma stems from fear, and fear stems from ignorance. Thanks to the work of charities like the Alzheimer's Society and individuals like Sir Terry and others in the public eye, dementia is in the news more than ever before. In February 2009, the government published *Living Well with Dementia: A National Dementia Strategy*, which sets out initiatives to improve the lives of people with dementia and their carers and families. With backing of £150 million over the first two years, the strategy includes proposals for more memory clinics, earlier diagnosis and interventions, and improvements in quality of care. It also aims to increase awareness of dementia.

Realistically, it is only when our own lives are touched that we tend to sit up and take notice, usually because we are filled with questions. I hope this book will go some way towards answering your own questions, that it will provide practical solutions to some of the difficulties that may arise, and that it will offer some support during what is likely to be a difficult time. I hope also that it will help you to feel comfortable discussing dementia, not only with your close friends and family but also with colleagues, neighbours and whoever else you happen to be chatting to. Talking freely about this all too common illness will help raise awareness, smash the stigma and improve the quality of life for all those living with its effects.

Note: Throughout the text, I usually refer to the person with dementia as 'your relative' or 'your loved one'; in most cases, the person with dementia will fall into these categories, but I hope you don't feel excluded if these terms don't really fit. I wanted to avoid repeating 'the person with dementia', partly because it's cumbersome, but mainly because it puts the emphasis on the illness rather than the individual. I have also avoided the overuse of 'he or she' and have instead alternated between the two.

1

What is dementia?

Dementia is the term used to describe a collection of symptoms that are caused by the destruction of brain cells as a result of certain diseases or conditions. Alzheimer's disease is the most common cause of dementia – more than half the people with dementia have Alzheimer's. The second most common cause is vascular dementia, which accounts for around 20 per cent of cases. Other fairly common causes are Lewy body dementia and frontal lobe dementia.

Dementia is a progressive disease, which means it will get worse over time. It usually begins in old age, but it is by no means an inevitable consequence of growing older. As we age, our memories, just like our bodies, become less robust, and we tend to forget things more easily than when we were younger. Mild forgetfulness is annoying but normal; the severe, life-affecting memory loss that characterizes dementia is not. It can be difficult to tell the difference in the early stages, but there are other symptoms associated with dementia that make it clearer that something is wrong. (See p. 8.) Although dementia is more common in older people, it can start earlier. There are currently around 15,000 people with dementia in the UK who are under the age of 65. Very rarely, it can start before the age of 40.

Alzheimer's disease

Alzheimer's disease is what we tend to think of when we hear the term 'dementia'. The name comes from the psychiatrist and pathologist Alois Alzheimer, who first described the disease in 1907 after noticing that protein deposits could be found in the brain of someone with dementia.

When your loved one is diagnosed, you may be told that he or she has 'dementia of the Alzheimer's type'. This is because a definite diagnosis of Alzheimer's disease can only be made by examining the brain tissue after a person has died. Doctors still don't know exactly what causes Alzheimer's, although it is thought there may be a genetic cause in a minority of cases (more about this on p. 6). However, the symptoms – the decline in the ability to remember, to learn, to think and to reason – are caused by physical changes in the brain which stop it from working properly.

When scientists examine the brain tissue of someone with Alzheimer's under a microscope, a number of changes can be seen. These include:

- small lumps called amyloid plaques, which grow in the areas of the brain responsible for controlling memory and thought. The lumps are made up of protein and parts of dead cells, and it is thought they may stop messages being passed between the brain cells;
- bundles of tangled threads, known as neurofibrillary tangles, which form inside the brain cells and prevent messages moving between them. They can also cause the cells to die;
- holes or gaps in brain tissue where cells have died;
- insufficient numbers of neurotransmitters (chemical messengers that move between the brain cells).

Myths about Alzheimer's

In the vast majority of cases, we don't know why someone develops Alzheimer's, and this lack of knowledge has led to a number of myths about the disease. We do know that Alzheimer's is definitely not caused by:

- overusing or underusing your brain;
- stress or bereavement;
- hardening of the arteries;
- contact with someone who has the condition; Alzheimer's is not infectious or contagious – it cannot be 'caught'.

There has been some circumstantial evidence linking Alzheimer's with aluminium. However, since the link was first suggested, there has been a great deal of research and no causal links have been identified. Aluminium is widely present in our environment, and we are all exposed to small amounts of it on a daily basis. Given that the majority of elderly people do not develop Alzheimer's, it is highly unlikely that it is a contributory factor.

Vascular dementia

Vascular dementia is caused by damage to the blood vessels in or near the brain. If the blood vessels are blocked or damaged, blood flow will be affected and this may result in a lack of oxygen to the brain, which in turn can damage or destroy some areas of brain tissue. Areas of brain tissue that have died through lack of oxygen are called infarcts. This is sometimes the result of a small stroke. Over time, several infarcts may appear and brain function will be affected, causing dementia. This is sometimes known as multi-infarct dementia. It is possible for Alzheimer's and vascular dementia to occur together.

Lewy body dementia

This is where small clusters of proteins called Lewy bodies form in the brain, affecting brain function. Lewy bodies are also found in people with Parkinson's disease, and some symptoms of Parkinson's – stiff muscles, a shuffling walk, loss of facial expressions – are sometimes seen in Lewy body dementia. As well as the usual dementia symptoms such as memory problems and confusion, people with Lewy body dementia may also experience hallucinations, and may have difficulty with balance.

Frontal lobe dementia

Frontal lobe dementia is where the damage to brain cells occurs in the front parts of the brain, which are the areas that control mood and behaviour. We don't yet know why this happens in some people. As with Alzheimer's, this type of dementia causes a progressive decline in mental function over a number of years, although the symptoms are slightly different in that the personality changes are very prominent, and may sometimes involve quite bizarre behaviour. The person may have trouble with language but, in the early stages, experience few or no difficulties with memory. This type of dementia tends to begin earlier than Alzheimer's, often when people are in their 40s or 50s.

Other causes of dementia

Dementia can also be caused by rarer diseases such as Korsakoff's syndrome, Binswanger's disease, Creutzfeldt-Jacob disease (CJD) and HIV and AIDS. Dementia may also be more common in people with motor neurone disease, Huntingdon's disease, Parkinson's disease and multiple sclerosis.

Who is at risk?

There is continuing research into why some people develop dementia and others don't. To a certain extent we're all 'at risk' of developing some form of dementia, but scientists have identified a number of factors that can increase that risk. It should be borne in mind that people who appear to have a high risk of developing dementia may never do so. It's also possible for the condition to develop in someone who appears to be at low risk.

Risk factors

Age

Age is by far the most significant risk factor. Some people develop dementia quite early in life, but it is relatively rare in people under 65. As we age, the risk increases. According to the Alzheimer's Society, only one in 1,000 people between the ages of 40 and 65 has dementia. This increases to one in 50 in those aged 65–70, one in 20 in 70- to 80-year-olds and one in five of those over 80. Other health conditions or illnesses associated with ageing may contribute to the increased risk: for example, conditions that affect the heart or blood vessels (the cardiovascular system) such as high blood pressure, heart disease and stroke.

Gender

Alzheimer's is slightly more common in women, while vascular dementia seems to affect men more than women. It has been suggested that the lack of the hormone oestrogen in post-menopausal women may be a factor in the development of Alzheimer's. However, studies show that taking hormone replacement therapy (HRT) does not lower the risk of developing the condition and, given the risks associated with HRT, it is not recommended as a protective measure. High blood pressure and heart problems are risk factors in vascular dementia, and given that these conditions are more common in men, this may explain why men are at greater risk of this type of dementia than women.

Family history

You may be concerned that because one of your parents or siblings has dementia you will be more likely to develop it yourself. It's true that someone who has a parent, sibling or child with dementia is slightly more likely to develop the condition, and the risk increases further if more than one family member is affected. However, it's not clear whether the reasons for this are genetic or environmental. Clearly, genetic factors (see below) are beyond our control, but environmental factors (see p. 7) such as diet, exercise and alcohol consumption are not, so you may be able to take steps now to reduce your own risk of developing dementia.

Genetics

Genes are the parts of a human cell that determine the characteristics that are passed down the generations from parent to child – curly hair, for example, or an aptitude for music. Research suggests that the genes we inherit from our parents may be partly responsible for whether or not we develop certain illnesses, including those that are known to be among the causes of dementia. However, there are almost 20,000 genes in the human genome, and although scientists don't know exactly how many of these genes play a part in the development of dementia, it could be over 100. So, even though the risk of developing dementia is slightly increased if you have a parent with the condition, it is unlikely that you will have inherited all the genes that would make you susceptible. In most cases, scientists believe dementia is caused by a combination of genetic and lifestyle factors so, in other words, even if someone inherits all the genes that would predispose him to dementia, it still doesn't mean he will definitely develop the condition.

There is one very rare form of Alzheimer's that does seem to have a strong genetic link. Scientists have identified three particular genes, known as APP, PSEN-1 and PSEN-2, that are associated with an early-onset form of Alzheimer's. People who have any of these rare genes tend to develop Alzheimer's while in their 30s and 40s, and will usually have several relatives with early-onset Alzheimer's. Only a small number of families in the world are affected, and the number of people with this form of Alzheimer's accounts for only 1 or 2 per cent of all Alzheimer's cases.

Medical history

Certain medical conditions can increase someone's risk of developing dementia. These include Huntington's disease, multiple sclerosis, HIV and Down's syndrome.

Down's syndrome

People with Down's syndrome are at significantly increased risk of developing dementia. One study suggests that around 2 per cent of people with Down's are likely to develop the condition in their 30s, rising to 9 per cent in their 40s, 36 per cent in their 50s and over half (54 per cent) by the time they reach their late 60s. Other studies have shown that almost all people with Down's develop the plaques and tangles in the brain (see p. 2) that are associated with Alzheimer's, though not all of them will develop the disease.

Environmental and lifestyle factors

It is thought that environmental and lifestyle factors can play a significant role in the development of dementia in some people. It is also true that a healthy lifestyle, both in terms of diet and exercise and in terms of social and intellectual stimulation, appears to help reduce the risk.

Alcohol

Drinking large amounts of alcohol over a long period of time can increase the risk of developing dementia. Heavy drinking can cause high blood pressure, which can damage the blood supply to the brain, starving it of oxygen and other vital nutrients. Also, alcohol is a toxin which causes direct damage to brain tissues. Very heavy drinkers may develop Korsakoff's syndrome (sometimes referred to as 'alcoholic amnestic syndrome'). This condition is not, strictly speaking, a true dementia, although people who have it will have problems with short-term memory. Korsakoff's syndrome can occur in non-alcohol-related conditions where there is severe malnutrition, but this is extremely rare in the UK. The condition is caused by thiamine deficiency. Heavy drinkers tend to have a poor diet, low in vitamins and other nutrients. Also, alcohol can damage the stomach lining, which can affect the body's ability to absorb any nutrients it does receive. Korsakoff's syndrome is more common in men with a history of heavy alcohol consumption, and tends to develop between the ages of 45 and 65.

Some studies have shown that a small amount of alcohol – one or two units a day – may actually protect against dementia. The type of alcohol may also be relevant, with some studies suggesting that wine is preferable to other types of alcohol. There is considerable evidence to suggest that small amounts of red wine, which contains anti-oxidants, may help to protect the heart and vascular system. We know that dementia is more common in people with a history of high blood pressure or heart disease, so this makes sense. But there may be other lifestyle factors that need to be taken into account: for example, people who prefer to drink wine may be less likely to smoke and more likely to have a healthy diet, whereas people who drink beer or spirits may be more likely to smoke and less likely to eat lots of fresh fruit and vegetables. It's difficult, therefore, to be certain about the links, but research into the subject continues.

Diet

We know by now that what we eat has a huge effect on our general health. A diet high in saturated fats can cause narrowing of the arteries, which can lead to heart attacks or stroke, and this in turn increases the risk of vascular dementia. We also know that if we eat a diet rich in fresh fruit and vegetables, we are more likely to have an adequate supply of vitamins and anti-oxidants, which may help to protect the brain and prevent disease of the heart and vascular system. Oily fish, a good source of polyunsaturated fatty acids, has also been shown to be beneficial to brain and cardiovascular health.

Smoking

Again, it won't be news to you that smoking is bad! Smoking damages the lungs, heart and blood vessels, including those in the brain. It can lead directly to stroke, which, as we've seen, increases the risk of vascular dementia.

Exercise

Physical exercise is vital to overall health, but particularly to cardiovascular health. Regular exercise helps to keep the cardio-vascular system healthy, reducing the risk of high blood pressure, heart disease and stroke, all of which are risk factors in vascular dementia.

What are the symptoms?

Although most people with dementia will have a number of symp-toms in common, each person's experience of the illness will be slightly different, and not everyone will have all the symptoms mentioned here. Dementia is a progressive illness, and in the early stages symptoms can be very subtle and difficult to spot, especially as they may be common to other illnesses. Some symptoms – a certain amount of forgetfulness, for example, or a tendency to repeat things – are normal and common consequences of ageing. Early symptoms may include:

- memory problems – forgetting appointments, recent events and dates, such as birthdays or anniversaries that the person usually remembers;
- repeating anecdotes and conversations;
- brief periods of appearing confused;

- denying problems or blaming others;
- becoming less adaptable and more unwilling than usual to try new things;
- overreacting to small problems.

It's often difficult to pinpoint the onset of dementia, partly because of the normal ageing process but also because there is a tendency to try and carry on as if nothing is wrong, particularly if the person becomes upset when loved ones mention their concerns. But if you have concerns about your loved one, you should talk to a doctor as soon as possible, both to rule out other possible causes for the symptoms (see p. 14) and to arrange for testing so that, if it is dementia, you can start thinking about planning the treatment and management of the condition. The next chapter looks more closely at the process of testing for and diagnosing dementia.

2

Diagnosing dementia

When should you seek help? As already mentioned, the early stages of dementia can be difficult to spot, but there will come a point at which your relative's behaviour leads you to consider dementia. You may have already noticed little lapses in memory and concentration, but these may progress and become more serious. There are some signs which, although they don't necessarily indicate dementia, could be symptoms of Alzheimer's, or of vascular dementia. These include:

- losing or misplacing things on a regular basis, or putting things in odd places – car keys in the fridge, for example – and then forgetting or denying having done this;
- difficulties with language – having trouble finding the right words, or substituting inappropriate words;
- disorientation about time and place – not recognizing familiar places, becoming confused about what time of day it is;
- decline in ability to assess certain conditions and situations: for example, dressing for winter on a hot summer's day, or being unaware of a dangerous situation such as a newspaper left near a gas fire;
- difficulty with familiar and often-repeated tasks: for example, forgetting the stages in making a meal;
- depression and mood problems such as irritability, agitation, apathy and lack of care with personal hygiene.

There may be other explanations for these symptoms, and there is probably no cause for alarm if your relative occasionally does something daft – we've all forgotten where we parked the car, or left the keys in the front door at least once. And it's not unheard of for a young, healthy person to be so busy trying to do a hundred things at once that he or she puts the steak in the waste bin and the packaging on to the grill pan. But if these things are beginning to happen regularly, or if your relative's behaviour puts her, or anyone else, in danger, now is the time to seek help.

Signs of Lewy body dementia

Symptoms of Lewy body dementia may be difficult to distinguish from those of Alzheimer's, in that they include short-term memory problems, depression and mood changes, and difficulties with concentration, reasoning and problem-solving. However, other symptoms that suggest Lewy body dementia are quite different. They include:

- visual hallucinations – seeing things that are not there, typically people, animals or children;
- non-visual hallucinations – hearing, smelling or feeling something that isn't there;
- body movements similar to those seen in Parkinson's disease, such as jerky movements or tremors, and muscle stiffness or rigidity;
- frequent falls or changes in the way the person walks – often a shuffling gait;
- dramatic fluctuation in mental function. This can be a bewildering situation for relatives. Typically, someone with Lewy body dementia may have periods of being alert and coherent, alternating with periods of confusion and unresponsiveness.

Getting a diagnosis

Diagnosing Alzheimer's is extremely difficult, and in fact it is often only after death that it is possible to be certain that someone has had the disease. There are many possible causes of dementia, however, and if someone is showing signs, it's important to seek medical advice without delay. The GP will be your the first port of call. He or she may know the family well, and your relative will hopefully feel comfortable explaining the difficulties she's been having. However, even if the GP is a family friend, people experiencing difficulties with mental function, especially when they know that these could be the symptoms of dementia, may feel embarrassed or ashamed, and may be reluctant to admit, even to themselves, that there's a problem. Sometimes, friends and relatives, especially husbands or wives, also find it hard to face the idea that their loved one may be developing dementia. As a result, they may cover up embarrassing behaviour or mistakes by putting it down to stress or tiredness. Couples who live together also tend to slot into each other's strengths and weaknesses even when there are no health problems, so when one partner begins to forget appointments the other is likely to make an extra effort, prompting or reminding so that the problems may take a long time to show up.

Why it's important to get a diagnosis

Some people have the idea that because there's no cure, there's no point in getting a diagnosis. But if someone seems to be showing signs of dementia it's important to seek help, for several reasons. First, although the condition cannot be cured it can be managed, and this can make life much easier for everyone involved. Dementia is a progressive illness, so it will become worse over time, and cognitive function will decline. An early diagnosis means that the person who has the condition will have the opportunity to take an active role in planning for the future. Your loved one may find it difficult to come to terms with the idea that, as time goes on, she will become increasingly dependent on others. This is a tough thing for everyone concerned to accept, but ignoring it will not make it go away, and facing it sooner rather than later means you will all have more time to think about the various issues, research the options and make decisions about the future as a couple or as a family.

Second, the sooner a diagnosis is in place, the sooner you will be able to access practical and financial help. There is a great deal of support and advice out there for people with dementia and their families. Unfortunately, some of it can be difficult to access, especially without a diagnosis. See Chapter 8 for more information about what help and support may be available.

Third, as the condition progresses, the person's behaviour may become more erratic and may even put him or her, or other family members or carers, at risk of harm. If your relative is behaving in a way that may put anyone in danger, seeking help should be a matter of urgency.

The first stage is to gently suggest to your relative that she might want to have a chat with her doctor about the difficulties she's been having lately. Offer to go with her to the doctor, either to just sit outside and wait, or to go in with her and help to explain what's been happening, if she feels that would help.

What if your relative insists there's nothing wrong?

If your relative says there's nothing wrong, try pointing out the things that are concerning you. Ask whether she genuinely thinks there's nothing wrong, or whether the truth is that she's worried that there may be a problem and is frightened about what it might be and what will happen as a result. Hopefully, you'll be able to offer some reassurance, perhaps by emphasizing that there are a number of possible causes for the symptoms and there may be a simple treatment. You should also point out that if this is the start of dementia, the sooner it is diagnosed, the sooner treatment to reduce the symptoms can be started (see Chapter 5) and the sooner you, as a couple or a family, can begin to make plans for the future.

It's worth being persistent when someone is refusing to see a doctor, because the person's mood may change from day to day, and you may find her more open to the idea at some times than at others. If it is your partner you're concerned about, another option is to suggest that you both go to the GP for an overall health check. You can then prime the GP first so that he or she is aware of your concerns.

If you cannot get your relative to the surgery, the doctor might be able to arrange a home visit in order to make an assessment about whether dementia is a possibility. In some cases, the GP may even prefer this, because it's sometimes easier to assess and observe people's behaviour when they're in their own home. If you think your relative is going to deny having any problems, it might be an idea to book an appointment with the doctor on your own first. Book the appointment in your relative's name so that the doctor has the notes to hand. Make a note of what you want to say when you get there, and of any questions you want to ask. Explain that your relative is sensitive about the situation – the doctor may have some advice about how to handle the whole thing diplomatically.

What will the GP do?

Once the GP understands the reasons for concern, the first thing he or she will do is to take a full history. This involves talking both to the person herself and to someone else who knows her well. This is usually a relative, but if you're a close friend and know more about what's going on than family members who might live some distance away, you're probably the best person for the doctor to talk to. The doctor will ask a lot of questions both about the symptoms and about the person's medical history. It's a good idea to make some notes before the appointment so that you can give as much information as possible. For example, it'll be useful for the doctor to know what the symptoms are, when they began and whether they came on suddenly or gradually over a period of some months. It might be helpful for the doctor to know if there's anything that seems to make things worse or better, and also what your relative's reaction to the symptoms tends to be: for example, is she distressed by them? Angry? Frustrated? Or does she insist there's nothing wrong?

This will usually be followed by a full physical examination. The doctor will also recommend a number of blood tests to check liver and kidney function, blood sugar and levels of thyroid hormone, cholesterol levels and the levels of vitamin B12 and folic acid. There is not, at the present time, any one test available that can confirm or exclude Alzheimer's, so the testing carried out at this stage is to try to establish whether there are any other health problems and any other possible explanation for the symptoms. Other possible causes of dementia-like symptoms include:

- Other illness – there are a number of other illnesses and conditions that may affect memory and brain function in general. These include chest infections, thyroid problems and depression. (See Chapter 5 for more about depression.) If another condition is causing the problems, treating that condition should bring about an improvement.

- Bereavement – sudden life changes such as bereavement can trigger severe depression, which can cause self-neglect as well as confusion and problems with memory and concentration.
- Alcohol and drugs – a combination of alcohol and drugs, even prescription medicines, can cause confusion. Sometimes even just a high dose of something like sleeping tablets may be responsible. Adjusting the dose, or ensuring the person avoids alcohol while taking the drug, can alleviate the symptoms.
- Physical disability – in some cases, a disability such as hearing loss or visual impairment can lead to what appears to be confusion and forgetfulness, simply because these disabilities make it more difficult for the person to absorb and register new information. This can lead to a relative thinking the person has forgotten something that happened or was said, when in fact she didn't actually see or hear it.

If the doctor suspects that your relative has dementia, or is developing the condition, he or she may make a referral to a specialist memory clinic for a more thorough assessment to confirm the diagnosis.

Tests to establish mental state

There are a number of mental function tests that can help towards a diagnosis of dementia. These may be carried out at your GP's surgery, at home or at a memory clinic, and may be carried out by a doctor or by a specialist nurse, usually a community psychiatric nurse (CPN). (The appendix at the end of the book has a list of healthcare professionals you may come into contact with during the process of diagnosis and treatment, together with a brief explanation of their roles.) Mental function tests usually involve a set of questions that are designed to show up difficulties with thinking processes, concentration and memory. These may include questions to establish the following:

- Orientation in time and place – the doctor may ask the person to say what day of the week it is, roughly what time of day, what the month is and the year, what the season is and what district they are in.

- Memory questions – these may involve asking the person to repeat a phrase or perhaps an address, then, after a few minutes have passed, asking her to repeat the words again. The doctor will explain beforehand that the question will be repeated, so the person will be able to make a conscious effort to remember.
- Concentration and calculation – this may be tested by asking the person to count back in sevens from 100 – 93, 86, 79, 72 and so on. The doctor will usually stop the test when the person gets to 65 or 58. If your relative has always had problems with numbers, tell the doctor. There are other tests that can be used: for example, counting back from 20 down to 1, spelling a word backwards or saying the months of the year backwards.
- Language skills – this may involve asking the person to name a common object such as a pen or a pair of spectacles, to write a sentence which must contain a subject and a verb and must make sense, and to follow a simple three-command instruction such as 'Take this piece of paper in the right hand, fold it in two, then place it on the floor.'
- Copying – the person is shown a drawing, which may be a simple three- or four-sided figure or a more complex shape, such as two pentagons which intersect to form a quadrangle, then asked to copy the same shape.
- Drawing a clock – this test involves asking the person to draw a clock face, putting in the numbers, and then drawing in the hands to show a particular time.

The doctor or nurse may carry out an assessment using the Mini Mental State Examination (MMSE), which consists of a number of tests like those listed above. The MMSE is popular because it only takes ten minutes or so to complete. The assessor will ask questions to test orientation, concentration, language, and registration and recall of information. The answers will be scored and the total used to indicate the level of cognitive impairment.

Once dementia has been diagnosed, the next stage will be to try and determine the cause. The vast majority of cases will be due to Alzheimer's disease or vascular dementia. More rarely, the cause is Lewy body, frontal lobe or other dementias. The likely cause of the dementia may have a bearing on how the illness will progress and the way it should be treated and managed.

3

After diagnosis

A diagnosis of Alzheimer's or other dementia can be a huge blow, even if it's what you expected. The realization that your relative has an illness that will get worse rather than better is obviously a difficult thing for you both to cope with, but it does mean that you now have the information you need to start planning for the future. It's important to make sure that he is able to maintain his independence and to continue to enjoy his usual activities for as long as possible. But it's also important to ensure that plans and arrangements for future care are not put off just because he is coping well at the moment. Dealing with the issues now means that the person concerned can consider the options and make decisions about the future while he still has the mental capacity to do so. Making plans now also allows time to research the best options and make absolutely sure that everyone concerned understands the wishes of the person who has the illness.

Some of the things you might want to consider are:

- What outside help is available?
- What costs might be involved and what benefits are available?
- Who is going to take care of his financial and legal affairs when he is no longer able to manage?
- Who is going to take responsibility for helping him with day-to-day living when these things become difficult?
- What support will be available for the person taking the main responsibility for day-to-day care?

You may find that your relative is reluctant to discuss these issues now, perhaps saying something like 'We'll cross that bridge when we come to it.' Try gently insisting that making plans isn't going to make the dementia progress more rapidly, but that ignoring potential problems could cause a lot of difficulty and upset later.

Money matters and legal affairs

Encourage your relative to put his financial and legal affairs in order as soon as possible. He may need help with this. Putting these issues off will mean that the task becomes more difficult for the person with dementia, and may mean that decisions are left to you or to other family members. If it's dealt with now, everyone will be clear about his wishes. For advice on financial and legal matters, it's worth contacting the Citizens Advice Bureau (CAB) (see Useful addresses). They may be able to help you resolve the problem or they may refer you to other sources of help; either way, they are a good starting point. Some CABs have their own solicitor, but if you need to find a solicitor yourself, talk to the Alzheimer's Society, who will be able to give you details of legal firms with specialist experience in dealing with legal issues related to dementia.

Some things that should be considered are:

Lasting power of attorney

A lasting power of attorney (LPA) is a legal process that allows an individual to give authority to another person to make a decision on his behalf. This allows the attorney to make decisions about financial and property matters, and about health care and personal welfare. Setting up an LPA means the person with dementia is able to choose someone he trusts to manage his affairs, and make his wishes known to that person while he still has mental capacity. The person with dementia can choose, if he wishes, to hand over responsibility for financial matters at any point, but LPAs relating to personal welfare can only be used once the person is no longer mentally capable. It's advisable to discuss this with a solicitor.

Benefits

There are a number of benefits that people with dementia and their carers should claim. Unfortunately, many of these remain unclaimed for various reasons, including reluctance to accept the diagnosis, anxiety about having to 'go into' financial matters or simply not being aware that these benefits are available. Chapter 8 has more information on claiming benefits, and also tells you where to get expert help and advice. It also explains about appointing an agent to collect benefits on behalf of the person with dementia, or an appointee to manage his income from benefits.

Domestic finances

Wherever possible, encourage or help your relative to set up direct debits to pay regular bills. Make sure that financial papers, including bank and building society statements, share certificates, mortgage statements, pension, tax and insurance details, bills and guarantees, etc., are roughly in date order and are kept somewhere where they can be found easily. Having a joint bank account can be very useful when someone is in the early stages of dementia, but once that person is no longer able to manage his financial affairs, the bank will probably want the accounts to be separate. It is also useful to have separate accounts in the later stages because, when it comes to considering care options, the local authority will carry out a means test, and this should only involve the finances of the person with dementia.

Making a will

Everyone should make a will, so if your relative hasn't already done so and still has the mental capacity, now is the time to do this. Anyone who dies without having made a will is said to have 'died intestate'. This means that the estate (money, property and possessions) will be divided up according to the law of intestacy – it will not, as most people assume, automatically go to the deceased's next of kin.

You may find it difficult to raise this subject, but there are ways! You could start by talking about making your own will and see what your loved one says. It may be that he's been meaning to make a will for some time but just hasn't got around to it, or it may be that he hasn't even thought about it. You could suggest that the two of you make your wills at the same time. If your relative already has a will that was made some time ago, he may wish to make changes. Either way, you should contact a solicitor as soon as possible. The solicitor, after taking medical advice, will decide whether the person with dementia still has 'testamentary capacity' – in other words, whether he is still capable of making legal decisions. Anyone who is deemed not to have testamentary capacity because of dementia will not be able to make or change a will, and no one else is able to do it on his behalf except, in certain circumstances, the Court of Protection, which may be able to make a statutory will. Your solicitor can explain this in more detail.

Living wills

Anyone over the age of 18 who has the mental capacity has the right to agree to or refuse medical treatment, and a living will is a way in which people can make their wishes clear while they still have the mental capacity to do so. The living will may include an 'advance decision', which is, in England and Wales, a legally binding refusal of certain types of treatment. The living will may also include an 'advance statement', which is a written statement of the person's general wishes, beliefs and attitudes or values. Although an advance statement is not legally binding, it can be used to help healthcare professionals and family and friends to make informed decisions on the person's behalf. It could include treatment the person would want to have and in what circumstances, treatment he'd prefer not to have and in what circumstances, and the name of someone he would like to be consulted if a decision needs to be made about his treatment. He could include something to say whether or not he would be happy for a new drug or treatment to be tried should one become available. He should also include: his full name and address, the name, address and telephone number of his GP, and whether he sought advice from a healthcare professional about making the statement. It's worth discussing this with the GP because he or she will be able to advise on the pros and cons of accepting or refusing certain treatments. The GP will also be able to confirm that your relative had sufficient mental capacity at the time he drew up the statement. When you and your loved one are satisfied that the statement is a clear representation of his wishes, the statement should be witnessed by an adult, who should not be the partner, spouse or relative of the person with dementia, nor his attorney under lasting power of attorney, nor anyone who stands to benefit under his will.

Driving

Your relative won't necessarily have to give up driving straight away after he has been diagnosed with dementia. However, there will come a point when driving will no longer be safe. Driving may seem like an automatic activity, especially when the person has been driving for many years, but in fact it is a complicated task requiring a number of complex thought processes and manual skills. In order to drive safely, we need to be able to 'read the road', make spilt-second decisions, anticipate what other drivers or pedestrians are going to do and respond quickly. And of course, we need to be able to take immediate decisive action to avoid accidents.

As dementia progresses, it affects memory, perception and the ability to carry out simple tasks. It is inevitable, therefore, that someone with dementia will have to stop driving when it can no longer be considered safe. The point at which this occurs will vary from person to person. Many people decide to stop of their own accord because they find driving has become stressful or confusing, whereas others find the idea upsetting and will only stop when they are legally required to do so.

Someone with a diagnosis of dementia must tell the Driver Vehicle and Licensing Authority (DVLA). They will send a questionnaire and a request for permission to contact the driver's doctor and/or specialist. The DVLA will then make a decision based on the medical information provided. They may ask the person to undertake a driving assessment, and if they are satisfied that the person's ability to drive is unimpaired, they will issue a licence, usually for a year, after which the situation will be reviewed regularly.

If your loved one is upset by the idea of having to stop driving, there are ways you may be able to help:

- Point out the possible alternatives to driving – buses, trains, taxis, the 'shoppers' bus', accepting a lift from a friend or neighbour, hospital transport.
- Point out ways of reducing the number of journeys: for example, shopping online so that the supermarket will deliver.
- Point out some benefits of not driving: for example, no more petrol costs or parking charges, no more tax, MOT, service and

repair bills. Travelling by public transport is usually much less stressful and can be more sociable. And not driving usually means more walking, which is good for health and fitness!

In some cases, the person with dementia is so upset by the prospect of not driving that he continues to do so, which is very worrying for friends and family. This is a very difficult situation and there are no easy answers. How to handle it will depend very much on the individual, but you may be able to get some useful advice from the Alzheimer's Society Dementia Helpline: 0845 300 0336.

How your loved one may feel

You would think that being told you have an incurable illness would be devastating, and for some it is, at least at first. However, for many people it marks the end of a long period of uncertainty, of knowing something was wrong but not knowing what. In some cases, the wait for an answer may have taken months or even years, possibly with a number of incorrect diagnoses along the way. To now have a tangible reason for the forgetfulness, the mood swings, the inability to do things they've done all their lives, can be an enormous relief.

Rose, a former maths teacher, now 62, was diagnosed with vascular dementia in 2006.

> I'd known something was wrong for more than two years before I was diagnosed. But I couldn't make the doctors listen. At first they said I shouldn't expect to be as 'on the ball' as I was when I was younger. They said it was natural to forget things now and again as I got older and that I was making things worse by worrying about it. But I knew it was more serious than that – I was quite regularly going completely blank in the middle of a conversation, and I knew that wasn't normal. My GP had already referred me to a psychiatrist, who told me I was depressed. I've suffered from depression in the past, so I know what that feels like and I knew this wasn't it, but my GP seemed determined to give me more antidepressants.
>
> Fortunately, my daughter came with me to the next appointment with my GP and demanded he refer me to a neurologist, which he did. I was glad to get the referral but I felt so frustrated at not being

listened to – I felt like I was going mad. The neurologist did several tests, including a brain scan, before telling me that I had vascular dementia. Even though it's a horrible illness to have, I was so relieved at getting a diagnosis that I just kept saying, 'Thank God for that!' which made them look at me as if I really *was* mad. But what it meant was that I could sit down with my daughter and my two sons and we could discuss what measures we might need to take in the future. It's not a nice thing to talk about, but it saves arguments later and everybody is clear about what I want to happen.

At the moment, I'm still coping quite well, especially now that Liz, my sister, has moved in with me to help out. But that won't be the case indefinitely, and I'm pleased that there's a plan in place for when things get too difficult. I do get a bit down about it from time to time – who wouldn't? But I'm concentrating on enjoying my life while I can. If a film comes on at the cinema that Liz and I fancy seeing, we go straight away, the same night if possible. Life's too short to put things off!

Rose was able to react positively to her diagnosis, but that's not the case for everyone. Your loved one may experience a number of different emotions, including anger, shock, resentment, anxiety, fear and grief. He may go through a stage of denial, and may appear so 'normal' and healthy that you all start to question the diagnosis. This is not uncommon. Dementia often progresses at different rates in different people and in different types of dementia. Also, the severity of symptoms can fluctuate, which can be misleading. Your relative is faced with the prospect of gradually losing his identity while he is still living. It is a difficult thing to face, and you shouldn't be surprised if this is a tough time for the whole family. You may both find it helpful to meet with or talk to other people with dementia, for example at an 'Alzheimer's Café'. These are café-style support groups, run by the Alzheimer's Society in many parts of the country. People with dementia and their loved ones can meet and socialize, compare notes and offer mutual support. From time to time, professional speakers come along to give a talk. Ask your local Alzheimer's society about this (see Useful addresses). You may find that people who've been living with dementia for a while can offer both of you advice and tips on coping with the diagnosis and on getting through the early stages.

How you may feel

How you react to your loved one's diagnosis will depend on a number of factors, including the nature of the relationship between you, whether you live in the same house, how much support you'll have from other family members, and so on. One thing is certain: your relationship will change as the illness progresses. The changes may be minor at first, barely noticeable, but gradually, often over a long period of time, his faculties will decline and you will inevitably shoulder more responsibility as a result. This can seem frightening, especially if you are very close and are likely to be the one who will be taking most of the responsibility for his care as well as, in many cases, the day-to-day running of the household. Try not to be too daunted by this. The decline often occurs very slowly, giving the whole family plenty of time to adjust and to make plans for managing the condition.

It's important to focus on the person, not the illness, and to make the most of the abilities he still has rather than simply mourning the decline of those he has lost. It's also important to try to understand how he's feeling. Given that dementia affects a person's ability to communicate, this can be one of the most difficult things to put into practice. Bear in mind that one of the biggest problems for someone in the earlier stages is frustration. Imagine what it must be like to put something down and then have no idea where you put it; to be completely unable to remember whether or not you have eaten lunch; to attend the birthday party of a beloved grandchild in the afternoon and have no memory of the event by evening.

In addition to the practical frustrations, there is the stigma to cope with. There is still such a stigma attached to dementia that not only are people reluctant to discuss it, but they are often reluctant to get a diagnosis. This seems to be the case with any illness that affects mental function; it's as though if we cannot *see* what's wrong, we can't possibly understand it.

Christine Bryden was diagnosed with a form of Alzheimer's disease in 1995 at the age of 46. Her illness made everything she did much more difficult and time-consuming, but she set about debunking the myths and raising awareness of the disease with a zeal that would put many fit and healthy people to shame. Despite being told she 'only had a few years', she continued to write and give talks and lectures on how it felt to live with dementia, right up until 2006, by which time she was exhausted and finding it too much. In her excellent and uplifting book, *Dancing with Dementia* (see Further reading, p. 113), Christine describes how reaction to the illness can affect the person with dementia:

> Daily tasks are more complex; nothing is automatic any more. Everything is as if we are first learning. Cooking burns, ironing is forgotten, washing is no longer sorted, and driving becomes scary. You tell us that we've asked you that question before, but we have no recollection. It is just a blank for the past. All this feels strange and scary, and yet you are frustrated with us. If we had an arm or a leg missing, you would congratulate us on our efforts.

Although it's important to keep in mind how the person with dementia is feeling, that doesn't mean you should neglect your own feelings, which may include anger and bitterness as well as sadness. As the condition progresses, it becomes difficult, and eventually impossible, to discuss the illness with your loved one. This can mean you feel lonely and isolated, especially when the person with dementia is your partner. See Chapter 10 for more about coping with difficult feelings.

Changing roles

Chapter 4 deals specifically with some of the problems that arise if the person with dementia is your spouse or life partner, but whether it's your partner, parent or other relative or friend, the dynamics of your relationship will change so that ultimately, you will take a more dominant role. This does not mean that you will 'dominate' the person with dementia, but it does mean that you will take more control than before, that you will perhaps 'take charge' of things that your relative was previously able to deal with without your help. Adjusting to these new roles can be challenging for both of you, but it is something you will both need to accept as soon as possible. How difficult the changeover will be depends a great deal on the roles you've each taken in the past. If your relative has always been the one to take the lead in the relationship, perhaps making many of the major decisions, or even just being the one to instigate most of the conversation, you may both find the shift a little more difficult than if it has been the other way around. It's important to remember that the transition will be gradual, giving both of you time to get used to the changes.

In his book, *Alzheimer's Early Stages*, Daniel Kuhn uses the analogy of ballroom dancers to explain this shift in roles:

> When a couple dances, the roles of the leader and follower are carefully orchestrated. A good leader dances in a way that enables the follower to be led almost effortlessly. The leader's cues may be so subtle that the follower may not appear to be led at all. The couple dances together gracefully as each partner cooperates in playing his or her part. In your relationship with a person with Alzheimer's Disease, you may be called on to change roles from follower to leader.

There are bound to be difficulties – it's a difficult situation – but hopefully, by arming yourself with as much information as possible, you'll be able to minimize these.

When the person with dementia is your parent

Whether we're 5, 25 or 55, there are times in our lives when we still think, 'I want my mum,' or 'I'm telling my dad.' On some level, we still want our parents to take care of us, to parent us. But when your parent has dementia, he or she can no longer take that role. As the condition progresses, you may find that there seems to be a complete reversal in roles so that it's almost as though you have become your parent's parent. It's important to remember that, although they may eventually need help even with what we regard as simple things such as washing, dressing or eating, people with dementia are not children but adults, with adult brains that are not functioning correctly because of an illness. A child has a capacity for learning and development that a person with dementia simply does not have; a child will become less dependent on his carers as he grows older, whereas a person with dementia will become more dependent. A person with dementia also has a lifetime's experience of love and loss, of success and failure, achievement and disappointment, as well as a lifetime of memories, many of which may still be accessible long after the memory of what happened ten minutes ago has gone. Bearing all this in mind will help you to help your parent maintain as much dignity as possible throughout his or her illness.

If you've always had a fairly good relationship with your parent, this will be much easier than if the relationship hasn't been so good. If there are still unresolved issues or conflicts between you, it is probably too late now to resolve them directly. This may be very frustrating – often, when we have problems in our relationships with our parents, we promise ourselves we will resolve them by confronting Mum or Dad, talking about how we feel, 'thrashing it out'. We will do this, we say, when the time is right. Feeling deprived of that option can lead to feelings of anger, resentment and even grief. If you find you're having trouble dealing with these perfectly understandable feelings, you should perhaps consider some counselling. Contact the British Association of Counselling and Psychotherapy (BACP) for more information and details of how to find a counsellor (see Useful addresses).

The extent to which you'll be involved will depend on whether both your parents are still alive and how able the healthy parent is to cope with the demands of having a partner with dementia. Some people are able to cope well at first, but need more and more support as time goes on; others are so upset by the diagnosis that they have difficulty coming to terms with it. In a few cases, an absolute refusal on the part of one or both parents to accept there is anything wrong can put a huge strain on the son or daughter who is trying to do the best thing for them. It can be frustrating if it's clear to the medical profession that your mum has dementia but your dad insists she's just getting a little forgetful.

Anne is a trained nurse, and when her father began having severe problems with his memory as well as difficulties with day-to-day living, she recognized the signs of dementia.

My dad is 84, but his memory has always been razor sharp, so it was very noticeable when he started forgetting things. At first, it was just forgetting to make phone calls or pay bills. Then I noticed he was repeating himself a lot, and he'd obviously started forgetting what people said to him – my mum would tell him she was popping out to the shops, then come back to find him furious because he thought she'd gone out without telling him.

I tried raising the subject with him, but he absolutely refused to acknowledge there was anything wrong, so I went round there one day when I knew he'd be out, and broached the subject with my mum. I was quite surprised when she also denied there was anything wrong, and seemed very upset and quite cross with me for suggesting it. Briefly, I wondered if I'd got it wrong, but things just got worse. He was leaving taps running, he was forgetting to shave or put his teeth in (unheard of!) and he could no longer dress himself without getting into a terrible mess.

I started going round every morning to help get him up and dressed, but it was difficult for me – I'm a lone parent and I work full-time – and it was also taking its toll on my mum. She's 81 and the tiredness and worry was making her ill, but she still denied there was anything wrong. In the end, I confronted her and she ended up in tears. It turns out she'd known for some time that there was something wrong, but she'd got it into her head that if she took him to the doctor or asked for help, he would be forcibly put in a home. She said she was afraid 'they'll take him away'.

Fortunately, I was able to put her mind at rest. I also persuaded her to come with me to talk to the GP about what was happening, and to let me contact social services. The GP diagnosed Alzheimer's, but Dad still doesn't know, and my mum is adamant that he mustn't be told. But at least they've got some help at home now – one carer comes every morning to get him up, and another comes in the evening to put him to bed. I pop round every day after work and help out at weekends. My mum looks much better now, and with the help of the carers, I think he'll be OK at home for a long time yet.

If your parents are resisting what seems obvious to you, don't waste your energy arguing about it at this stage; the most important thing is to make sure your parents are safe. So if your mum wanders during the night or lights the gas under the electric kettle, this is what needs to be addressed, rather than whether she does or doesn't have dementia. Because of the history of the parent–child relationship, your parent might resent what he sees as interference on your part. This is where outside help is useful. You may be able to enlist the help and support of your siblings if you have them (see below). This means you can at least present a united front, although you might need to labour the point that you are all acting out of concern. If you're the only one, or your siblings live too far away, is there anyone else in the family who could support you? Or maybe your parents have friends or neighbours who might be prepared to help. Sometimes a gentle suggestion from their peers may be easier to take on board than what they see as nagging from their children.

Siblings

Whether your relationship with your parent was good or bad, finding yourself in the position of the main carer can be demanding and challenging. If you have siblings, you would hope to share the workload, but in practice much of the responsibility usually falls to one person, either because he lives nearer to the parent, or he is deemed (by the other siblings) to have fewer domestic responsibilities of his own. Try to make sure your siblings take at least some of the responsibility. Even if they live too far away to do the shopping or take your parent to medical appointments on a regular basis, perhaps they could take care of some of the admin. Or perhaps they could come to stay for a few days so you can have a break, or have your parent stay with them for a while. The best way to sort out who's doing what is to call a family conference so that everyone knows what the current situation is and how much help your mum or dad needs. It's possible that your siblings, especially if they don't see your parent very often, may think you are exaggerating the illness and the amount of help and support required. If this happens, it may be worth asking your GP or community psychiatric nurse (CPN) to come along to the meeting to help explain the situation. This would change the dynamics of the meeting, so that it's not you asking your siblings for help, it's a healthcare professional explaining the needs of an individual to that person's family.

How much help?

Deciding how much help your relative needs can present quite a challenge, especially as the symptoms of dementia can fluctuate considerably. One day, your loved one is perfectly able to cook Sunday lunch for four people; the next, he can't remember how to make a cup of tea. This can lead to frustrations on both sides. For example, on a 'good' day, you may wonder whether the diagnosis was mistaken – your relative looks healthy, is coping well with his usual routine, can follow the conversation, even remembering (better than you can!) the names of half the cast of that film you both saw last year. So you start to think maybe it's not dementia, maybe it was something minor and it's better now. And then a couple of days later, he decides to do some ironing, but forgets halfway through and starts vacuuming instead, leaving the iron scorching its way though the duvet cover. Obviously, you want to be able to provide as much help as he requires, but this is something that needs to be constantly reassessed. From the point of view of the person with dementia, it can be frustrating because he is trying to remain as independent as possible, and probably doesn't want to 'be a burden'. But on the other hand, he wants to feel safe and supported, and if he appears to be coping very well with day-to-day tasks, it's easy to overlook this.

Janet's mum, Doreen, is 83 and was diagnosed with Alzheimer's six years ago. She now lives in a residential home that specializes in caring for people with dementia.

Mum coped well for quite a while after her diagnosis. She'd been a school dinner lady when she was younger, and she loved being in the kitchen. She continued to help out with the cooking at her senior citizens' lunch club, and she still did most of her own shopping and cooking at home for some time after being diagnosed. To be honest, I did wonder whether they'd made a mistake. She'd forget things, but then so do I; what I didn't realize was just how bad it was getting, especially as she seemed so independent. She'd get quite cross with me if I tried to do things for her, especially if it was anything cooking-related. The only thing she eventually agreed to let me do was to write out recipes. She got very frustrated that she couldn't remember how to cook things she'd been making for years, but she could still follow the recipes at first. I knew her memory was getting worse. Sometimes she'd forget to get dressed and would still be in her nightie when I called in on the way home from work, but she'd laugh about it so it still didn't seem that serious.

It was only when she started forgetting to eat, or making inedible meals – adding ingredients three or four times or leaving them out completely because she'd forgotten what she'd done already – that I realized just how bad things had become. It was then that I started paying more attention to other things. I hadn't really looked around the house properly, for example, and I was quite shocked. Upstairs was very dirty and untidy, and I kept finding things in strange places – things Mum was convinced she'd lost or that someone had stolen. She hadn't paid bills, hadn't even opened the letters.

It upset me when I realized the state she was in. I should have seen it before, but because she seemed to cope so well with some things, I was blind to the rest of it. I think I was kidding myself that she didn't really have dementia. Once I realized how bad things were, my sister and I took turns to stay with her so that she was never alone, but as things got worse we made the decision to go for residential care, where she's been for nearly two years now. These days, she doesn't recognize me or my sister when we visit, but in general she seems happy, and she sings a lot – she can still remember all the words to songs that she used to sing when we were children!

What Janet describes is a fairly typical situation, and she shouldn't blame herself for not realizing how her mother's condition was progressing. Sometimes, when people are coping well with some things, it's easy to overlook what else is happening, especially when the person seems so well. One of the most difficult things with dementia is that people who have it often look and seem perfectly healthy, and may argue very strongly with you if there's any suggestion that they're struggling to cope.

This is a matter that should be discussed at an early stage if possible.

4

When the person with dementia is your partner

How dementia will affect your relationship will depend to a large extent on how you and your partner managed your relationship in the past. If you have always taken more of a leadership role, or if you and your partner have taken fairly equal roles, you will probably adapt more easily than someone who was more the follower. Likewise, if you have built a close, loving and solid partnership together, you are likely to be able to cope with the problems dementia will throw at you a little more easily than couples who may have had a less settled or more turbulent relationship. But even if you've been married for ever, have a rock-solid relationship and are very used to taking responsibilities, it still won't be easy, especially as the condition progresses and communication becomes difficult. This can mean you feel very alone. If you and your partner are not very close, or if you've had an unhappy marriage, the prospect of having to care for that person can be very daunting.

A marriage or similar partnership flourishes when each party is able to nurture the other, encouraging their dreams and ambitions, sharing their disappointments as well as their joys. In addition, the practical side of the couple's life together will be shared. Whether things are shared equally or not, there will probably be certain chores and responsibilities that each partner regards as his or her 'job'. When dementia hits, this must change. So, for example, if you've always been the one responsible for the household admin, the decorating and the cooking, while your partner took care of the garden, the laundry and the shopping, you will gradually have to take on more and more of those tasks you've never had to worry about before. Clearly, this will be gradual – your workload won't double overnight – but you may have to learn new skills in order to carry out tasks you thought you'd never have to concern yourself with. Sadly, it is inevitable that your life will become busier and more complicated as a result of your partner's dementia, so the thing to do now is to look at how you can minimize the negative impact of these changes. It's important to try and understand your partner's increasing limitations and to work with them. Then you need to take practical steps. Some things that might help are:

- Get your partner to talk you through certain tasks while she is still able to do them.
- Write down the details of those tasks so you don't forget them – with so much to think about, you're quite likely to have the odd memory lapse yourself!
- Decide which jobs you have to do yourself, and which can be delegated. Maybe a family meeting and a rota system have a part to play. If you don't have family nearby, maybe your neighbours might be interested in a 'skills swap': for example, mowing the lawn in return for a homemade casserole, or doing the weekly shop in return for having the guttering cleared.
- Work out ways of minimizing the things that have to be done. For example, if your garden has a lawn that needs cutting, could you redesign the garden so that you have a paved terrace and a gravelled area instead? If you pay your utility bills by cheque or credit card, could you set up direct debits so that you don't have to actually do anything in order to pay the bill?
- Might you be able to pay someone to do jobs your partner has always done, such as cleaning windows, ironing, washing the car, etc.?

Sex and intimacy when your partner has dementia

Dementia causes changes in all areas of life, and is very likely to cause changes in your sex life. This is an area that tends not to be talked about – our society seems to deny the sexuality of people who are elderly and/or ill. It's true that some couples find that the sexual side of their relationship becomes less important as they get older, especially if they become ill. But for many people, sexual closeness continues to be a desirable and enjoyable aspect of their relationship well into old age and despite ill health. The onset of dementia doesn't have to mean the end of an active sex life, but you should be prepared for some changes in this, as in other areas of your relationship.

The diagnosis itself can have an impact on your sex life. On the plus side, it may explain problems and difficulties you've been having – things you may have thought indicated a problem in your relationship but that you can in fact put down to the illness. Alternatively, the confirmation that your partner has dementia may cause you both to experience negative emotions such as anger, anxiety, resentment, guilt, fear and, of course, sadness and grief. It's perfectly normal to feel this way – after all, the situation is an upsetting one. But now is the time to draw on the strengths of your relationship and talk about how you're both feeling. Try to share your worries, your thoughts and your fears about the future. As the illness progresses, verbal communication will become more difficult, and it may be that physical intimacy becomes an even more important method of communication and a rich source of mutual pleasure and comfort.

The brain controls sexual feelings, manners and inhibitions, so sexual behaviour is likely to be affected, but many people with dementia continue to have a happy and fulfilling sex life for many years. Most couples achieve this by recognizing that there are likely to be changes, and learning how to adapt to them. The nature of these changes will depend on which part of your partner's brain is affected, and what medication he or she is taking. Changes may include:

- having less or no interest in sex;
- having more interest in sex;
- being more or less able to 'perform' sexually;
- being more or less inhibited than usual;
- seeming to ignore good sexual 'manners' – for example, appearing insensitive to your feelings and needs, or seeming selfish or even aggressive in bed;
- displaying odd or inappropriate sexual behaviour.

So, how do you deal with these problems?

Loss of interest in sex

Diminished libido is very common in people with dementia, as are erectile dysfunction in men and problems with vaginal dryness in women. What is not certain is whether these problems are entirely due to brain damage caused by dementia or whether they may be a psychological reaction to the diagnosis. Some couples are fairly happy for this side of their relationship to be less active as long as closeness and affection are maintained. Problems can arise when one partner wants to have sex and the other doesn't. Clearly, this is a problem for any couple, not just those who are living with dementia. Often, the desire for sex is a representation of the need for people to feel loved and wanted, to feel highly prized by their partner and to feel secure in their affections. It may be that if you increase the physical closeness between you – touching, stroking, kissing, cuddling, holding hands and so on – your desire for sexual activity will diminish; but if it doesn't, it's important to recognize this and not to feel guilty about it. A build-up of sexual tension can make you feel frustrated and uncomfortable, and may cause you to resent or feel angry with your partner, even though you know the loss of desire is linked with dementia rather than indicating some problem between you. Physical exercise and/or masturbation can help relieve this tension and is a good practical solution.

Increased sexual desire

It's not unusual for someone with dementia to experience an increase in desire, and some partners may be delighted about this. However, if the increased interest is not so welcome, it can lead to problems. For example, you may be afraid to show normal affection such as hugging or kissing your partner in case he interprets it as a sexual overture. If you find your partner's sexual demands too much to cope with, one possible solution is to try to find something else to do together so that you're still demonstrating affection. Of course, this may not be easy if your partner is reaching for you in bed at night, but it may still be possible.

Sometimes, people with dementia can become uncharacteristically sexually aggressive, even violent. If this happens, try to stay out of your partner's way until the mood has passed. Often, as the illness progresses, the person becomes calmer. But if aggressive behaviour becomes a serious problem, or if you are unable to cope, seek advice from your doctor or consultant. It is sometimes possible to prescribe medication in cases like this, although this is usually considered a last resort.

Difficult or challenging sexual behaviour

Because dementia affects the brain, your partner's behaviour during or after sex may be very different to how it was before the illness became apparent. Some people with dementia may appear withdrawn and detached during sex; they may forget that they have had sex immediately afterwards, or they may appear to not recognize their partner. Because sex is such a personal and intimate activity, something you've probably shared, enjoyed and giggled about together for many years, any of these scenarios can be terribly upsetting, and may give the impression that your partner is being selfish and unfeeling, or that he or she no longer cares about you. Some people have said that having sex with their partners who have dementia makes them feel like objects or 'a piece of meat'. Even though you may understand and accept rationally that the dementia is to blame, this doesn't make it much easier to deal with. If this happens to you and you find it upsetting, you should seek support to help you come to terms with what's happening. Contact the Alzheimer's Society (see Useful addresses) to talk it through with one of their support workers.

Dementia can cause people to lose their inhibitions, which can lead to inappropriate or even aggressive or violent sexual behaviour. Again, it's helpful to remember that this is the dementia talking, rather than the person with the illness, but the most important thing is to keep yourself safe. If your partner is physically stronger than you and tries to use force to make you have sex, or if you find that you are agreeing to sex because you are frightened of what your partner might do if you refuse, you should seek outside help rather than trying to cope on your own. Talk to your GP or contact the Alzheimer's Society Dementia Helpline (0845 300 0336) for confidential advice.

Loss of sexual inhibitions can cause your partner to behave inappropriately in other ways, perhaps talking about or displaying sexual feelings in public. People with dementia may start to undress, touch themselves, or perhaps approach people other than their partners in a sexual way. They may simply mistake someone else for their partner. This behaviour can be upsetting and embarrassing, and may be very distressing and frustrating for your partner, who probably has no idea why her behaviour is considered inappropriate. If this is the case, try to reassure your partner while gently discouraging the behaviour, perhaps leading her towards a different activity. Also, it's worth remembering that some behaviour that appears to be sexual – undressing, touching him- or herself, etc. – is in fact an indication of something else entirely. It may simply mean that your partner needs to use the lavatory, is too hot, is itching or is finding some item of clothing too tight. Try to find out what is causing the behaviour before interpreting it as sexual. See Chapter 6 for more about coping with unusual or difficult behaviour.

How your own feelings may be affected

As your partner's dementia progresses, you may find that you feel less like having sex. This may happen for a number of reasons.

Tiredness

Having a partner with dementia can be physically and mentally exhausting, even if you have some help with caring. If this is the case, try to reassure your partner by showing affection in other ways. It may be that having a short break by organizing some respite care now and again (see p. 84) will enable you to rest and recover sufficiently to be able to revive that side of your relationship, even if it happens infrequently.

Personal care

If you are the main carer, you may find that some of the intimate tasks you have to perform as part of your partner's daily routine – washing, dressing, toileting, and so on – put you off the idea of sex. This is one of the difficulties that often arises as a result of the change in your relationship from equal life partners to 'carer' and 'cared for'. You may feel it is your duty to attend to your partner's personal needs, but you've probably already taken on a massively increased workload as a result of your partner's illness, so if it's at all possible to get outside help with these tasks (see p. 80) it's worth considering and may allow you to feel more like life partners once more. Sometimes just the fact that you have a role as your partner's carer can change the sexual dynamic between you. After all, the word can become something of a label, and also has connotations of parenting. One way of dealing with this may be to make sure that your role as life partner takes precedence. For example, if you have had to perform a number of 'caring duties' in the morning, make sure you do something together as a couple in the afternoon, even if it's only going for a walk and perhaps stopping somewhere for a coffee. Accentuate your coupledom, and if outside help with personal care isn't an option, use humour to deal with difficulties where possible. It may also help to talk to a support worker about this aspect of coping with dementia. Contact the Alzheimer's Society for advice.

Changes in your partner's behaviour

As we have seen, dementia can cause people's sexual behaviour to change, causing odd, clumsy, insensitive or even aggressive behaviour. Some people say that they feel they are having sex with a stranger rather than making love with their life partner. Clearly, this makes it difficult to enjoy a sexual relationship. Try to remember that it is the illness that causes these changes, and that your partner may not understand why his or her behaviour is inappropriate. He or she may be confused and distressed by your reaction, so try to find other ways of being intimate together. If you find your partner's sexual behaviour upsetting or distressing, don't be tempted to grit your teeth and put up with it – this will only lead to resentment and won't help either of you in the long term. It may help to talk things over with a support worker.

If you are having difficulties in your sexual relationship, you may decide to move to a separate bed or a separate room. Your partner may not understand why this is happening and may be disorientated or distressed by this. Again, it's a good idea to talk this through with a dementia support worker.

If your feelings stay the same

Some people find that their feelings towards their partner remain virtually unchanged, and that they are able to continue a loving sexual relationship despite the progression of the illness. For couples who continue to enjoy the physical side of their relationship, sexual intimacy becomes increasingly important as other forms of communication become more difficult. You may find that it becomes a vital way of connecting with your partner, cherishing each other as you have done throughout your life together.

However, even if your feelings for your partner haven't changed, difficulties may arise if he or she is unable to communicate verbally and seems unresponsive during sex. You may worry that your partner didn't really want to have sex, and this can make you feel guilty, as though you are taking advantage of the fact that your partner is unable to make his or her wishes clear. If this happens, it's important to pay close attention to your partner's body language. Be aware of non-verbal signs, and stop if there's any sign of reluctance.

Maintaining a sex life when your partner is in residential care

If your partner lives in, or is soon to move to, a residential or nursing home, you may be concerned that this heralds the end of your sex life. Just because people are elderly or have an illness, it doesn't change the fact that they are sexual beings, and they have an equal right to express their sexuality. Talk to the manager of the home and explain that you and your partner would like to have some private time together on a regular basis. Ask how this might be arranged. You may also want to ask whether the home has a sexuality policy, and what training staff members have on relationship matters. For example, if a resident were to become confused and make a sexual approach to another resident or a staff member, how would they handle this?

Staying positive

It's clear that dementia can have a devastating affect on relationships, but there is a great deal you can both do to keep your relationship healthy. Spending time apart as well as together will give you both a break – your partner may feel guilty for being a 'burden' and so may welcome the chance to relax in the knowledge that you are having some time to yourself. If it's no longer safe for your partner to do things alone, see if a friend or relative can help out now and again.

When you are together, try to make sure you factor in some social and 'fun' time, as well as coping with your daily routine. Seeing friends together, going for a walk, a meal or to the cinema, or simply looking through photo albums together can reaffirm your existence as a couple. Taking part in activities and pursuits you've always enjoyed can boost your self-esteem and provide a valuable outlet for the frustrations you both feel as a result of the illness.

5

What treatments are available?

There is no cure for dementia at present, but there are some medications developed specifically for Alzheimer's disease that may help improve symptoms such as memory problems, wandering, and aggressive behaviour. There are also a number of non-drug treatments and therapies that may improve the symptoms of other types of dementia as well as Alzheimer's.

Drugs for Alzheimer's

There are two main types of drug used to treat Alzheimer's disease. They can help improve symptoms or slow the progress of the disease in some people:

Aricept, Exelon and Reminyl

These drugs are known as acetylcholinesterase inhibitors. They work by preventing the breakdown of a brain chemical called acetylcholine. Higher concentrations of acetylcholine facilitate increased communication between the nerve cells that use it as a chemical messenger; this in turn can temporarily improve the symptoms of Alzheimer's disease. Although these three drugs work in the same way, one may be more suitable for a particular individual than another. The treatment needs to be started by a consultant, so a GP should refer your relative to the hospital for tests to establish whether this would be an appropriate course of action. If your relative is suitable, the consultant will write the first prescription, and after that your GP will be able to prescribe the drug.

Studies suggest that around half the people with early or middle-stage Alzheimer's who take acetylcholinesterase inhibitors experience some improvement in their symptoms. Benefits include improved memory, thinking and concentration, increased motivation and confidence, and a reduction in anxiety. The person's ability to carry out household tasks and personal care may improve, and he may seem generally more 'on the ball'. These drugs are not effective for everyone, however, and for some the improvements are temporary.

At the time of writing (2009) these drugs are licensed for people with mild to moderate Alzheimer's. However, guidelines from the National Institute for Clinical Excellence (NICE) changed in 2006 to recommend that they should be available as an NHS treatment only for people with moderate Alzheimer's. These guidelines are currently being reviewed. There is increasing evidence to suggest that these drugs may be effective in people whose symptoms are more severe, but they are not currently licensed for this. It may be possible to get Aricept, Exelon or Reminyl privately, but there will also be consultation fees, prescription charges and dispensing fees, so the cost may be prohibitive. Whether the drugs are obtained through the NHS or privately, they should only be used after full consultation with the doctor.

Bob was prescribed an anti-dementia drug as soon as he was diagnosed with Alzheimer's disease in 2004, before the NICE guidelines changed.

I was 66 when I got the diagnosis, and I was in a bad way. My memory was so poor that I couldn't go out on my own because I'd forget how to get home. I couldn't watch a film on the television because I couldn't follow the plot – I used to drive my wife mad because I had to keep asking her what was happening. And it would take me a week to read one page of a book, because I had to keep going back to the beginning. We both knew something wasn't right, so we went to the doctor together. He did a few tests and said what I was afraid he'd say – that I had Alzheimer's. But he put me on Exelon straight away, and within a few weeks it was like I was a different person. It was as though I could feel the fog clearing from my brain. Things started to make sense again; it made a huge difference. Fortunately, because my GP prescribed the pills before the guidelines changed, I still get my pills on the NHS – we couldn't afford it privately. I know I'm not 'cured', but at the moment I'm coping. I can go to the shops, I can watch a film, I can even read a book without having to go back to remind myself what's happened. I dread to think what I'd be like by now if I wasn't taking the pills.

Ebixa

Ebixa works by blocking the action of glutamate, a chemical messenger that is released in large quantities when brain cells have been damaged by Alzheimer's disease. These high levels of glutamate cause yet more damage to the brain cells. Ebixa stops this from happening by preventing the release of excess glutamate. Ebixa is licensed for the treatment of moderate to severe Alzheimer's, and can temporarily slow down the progression of the symptoms in people in the middle and later stages of the disease. However, this drug is not routinely available through the NHS.

Side effects

Few side effects have been reported for any of these drugs, which all seem to be tolerated fairly well. If side effects do occur with Aricept, Exelon or Reminyl, the most common include nausea, vomiting, diarrhoea, stomach cramps, headaches, dizziness, insomnia and loss of appetite. Side effects of Exiba include headaches, dizziness, tiredness, raised blood pressure and, rarely, hallucinations and confusion. Exiba may not be suitable for everyone, especially people with kidney or heart problems, or epilepsy.

Stopping drug treatment

If a person has been taking these drugs and then stops, his or her condition will deteriorate over the following four to six weeks. The symptoms will gradually return or become more severe until they will start to affect the person just as if she had never taken the drug. If your relative wants to stop taking the drugs she's been prescribed, perhaps because of troubling side effects, encourage her to talk to the doctor first – there may be a simple solution.

Drugs for other dementias

Acetylcholinesterase inhibitors were developed specifically to treat Alzheimer's disease, but there is some evidence to suggest that they may be effective in Lewy body dementia and in dementia associated with Parkinson's disease, and indeed Exelon is licensed for this purpose. Research is continuing to examine the effectiveness of these drugs in the treatment of vascular dementia, but the benefits appear to be few, except in people who have Alzheimer's as well as vascular dementia.

Other drugs that may be prescribed

It's generally agreed that someone with dementia should take as few drugs as possible, but if the person develops behavioural problems such as aggression, severe anxiety or restlessness, or psychiatric symptoms such as hallucinations or delusions, it may be that some form of medication is appropriate. Before this option is considered, it's important to try to find the underlying cause for what is happening. If your relative is anxious, restless or seems aggressive, could there be a physical cause? Might she be in pain or discomfort from an unnoticed injury, infection or other medical condition? Something as simple as an ingrown toenail or a blister can cause considerable pain, and any untreated pain or illness can affect the person's behaviour. Could she be having problems with her hearing or eyesight? Being unable to hear properly can cause someone with dementia to become more confused than usual, and poor eyesight can be at least partly responsible for the development of visual hallucinations. If she is unable to articulate these difficulties, the effects on her mood and behaviour can easily be misinterpreted. These areas should all be investigated and any problems treated before other medication is considered.

Depression

Depression is a serious illness that needs to be treated. When someone becomes depressed, there are often a number of contributory factors. These may include bereavement or other loss, life changes such as retirement or moving house, worries about money, relationships or family problems, illness, side effects of medication, loneliness, isolation or boredom. In someone with dementia, this list may also include worries about memory loss and fears for the future, as well as chemical changes in the brain that are caused by the dementia.

Depression is very common in older people, and people with dementia tend to be more prone to the condition. It can be difficult to diagnose, especially as the symptoms are so similar to those of dementia, which means that sometimes people who have dementia may be misdiagnosed as having depression, and people with depression may be mistakenly thought to have dementia. Dementia and depression are both conditions that can affect people's ability to articulate their feelings, so this makes it even more difficult to make an accurate diagnosis. However, close observation should show up some of the differences between depression and dementia. For example, someone who is depressed may complain of having a poor memory but is often able to remember things when prompted, whereas someone with dementia is likely to try to cover up memory lapses. Although someone with severe depression may appear confused as a result of poor concentration, there are unlikely to be serious problems with speech, reasoning and orientation in time and space, whereas someone with dementia may experience considerable impairment in these areas. Severe depression can affect reasoning and memory, but when the depression lifts or is treated, this is reversed and the person's reasoning skills and memory return to normal. This does not happen with dementia.

It is not uncommon for someone to become depressed as a consequence of dementia. In the early stages, this may be a reaction to the diagnosis of dementia, or it may have something to do with changes in brain chemicals. Whatever the cause, it means that the person will be coping with two life-affecting conditions. Depression can exacerbate the dementia symptoms, causing the person to appear more confused, anxious, forgetful or withdrawn, or it can make him agitated, restless and even aggressive.

If you are concerned that your relative's behaviour may indicate depression, or if the symptoms of dementia seem to be getting worse more rapidly than you expected, talk to your GP as soon as possible. There may be other causes, such as illness, infection or side effects to medication, and these need to be ruled out in order to make a diagnosis. As well as carrying out a physical examination, the doctor will, if possible, talk to your loved one as well as to you and other carers or relatives about the changes in his behaviour or mood. Symptoms vary a great deal from person to person, but the doctor may ask questions such as:

- Does your relative seem lethargic or listless?
- Does he appear more anxious or agitated than usual?
- Is he often tearful?
- Does he wake early or have trouble getting to sleep?
- Does he sleep more or less than usual?
- Does he seem unable to experience pleasure or enjoyment?
- Does he complain of feeling sad, bleak or hopeless?
- Have there been changes in his appetite?
- Has he lost interest in friends, relatives and social activities he would normally enjoy?

What treatments are available?

Treatments for depression include psychological therapies, anti-depressant medication and social support. If the person has fairly mild symptoms of depression or anxiety, formal treatment such as drugs or counselling may not be necessary. In some cases, the person's mood improves with extra support and attention. If your loved one is feeling vulnerable and anxious about the future, she may just need some reassurance and friendly interaction such as talking or hand-holding. Minor changes in her daily routine may help: knowing that there will be a regular daily visitor, for example; activities such as a walk or other outing; or simply having a more reassuring structure to each day.

For someone whose dementia is not too far advanced, psychological interventions such as counselling or cognitive behaviour therapy (CBT) might be appropriate, possibly combined with anti-depressant medication.

- Counselling – there are many different types of counselling, and some of these may be available through your GP's surgery. Talk to your doctor about what types of counselling are available and whether they might be appropriate for your relative.
- Cognitive behaviour therapy – depression, low mood or anxiety can sometimes occur as a result of certain ways of thinking. CBT works by identifying these negative thoughts and then helping the person to adjust his thought patterns so that they become less negative. CBT is often available as an NHS treatment.

- Support groups – many people find that talking to others in a similar situation can provide great comfort and support. Contact your local branch of the Alzheimer's Society for details of local dementia support groups.

Antidepressants

Antidepressant medication is generally a safe and effective treatment for depression, provided the treatment is closely monitored and the medication is taken according to the doctor's instructions. Most of the problems reported with this type of treatment occur as a result of the dose being too low, the person not taking the drug regularly or for a long enough period of time, or the medication being stopped too abruptly.

If your relative is prescribed antidepressants, try to ensure that he takes them regularly, as prescribed. It can take two or three weeks for the drugs to start working, and there may be some side effects as the body adjusts, but these usually settle down quite quickly. The doctor should monitor the treatment very closely at first in case the dose needs to be adjusted or the type of drug needs to be changed. It is usually recommended that antidepressants should be taken for at least six months after the person last had symptoms of depression. Some experts say it should be even longer – nine months to a year – in order to reduce the risk of symptoms returning. When coming off antidepressants, the dose should be gradually reduced over a period of a few weeks; stopping suddenly can cause symptoms to resurface.

There are many different types of antidepressants, and some people may find the first one they try doesn't work. Some people will try two or three different types or brands before finding one that is effective for them. Some types of antidepressants that may be prescribed include selective serotonin re-uptake inhibitors (SSRIs), which are widely used and are effective for many people. They may have some side effects, but these tend to be tolerated more easily than those of other antidepressants. Some commonly prescribed SSRIs are: Prozac, Seroxat, Cipramil, Faverin and Lustral. Other classes of antidepressant, including Zispin and Edronax, may also be prescribed for someone with dementia. You may wonder why your doctor doesn't try certain other types of antidepressant, such as tricyclic antidepressants or monoamine oxidase inhibitors (MAOIs). This is because these drugs, although they may be effective antidepressants, would not be suitable for someone with dementia. Tricyclic antidepressants, including Lentizol, Tofrinol, Dothiepin and Prothiadenor, can have troublesome side effects including blurred vision and drops in blood pressure, and can cause confusion even in older people who don't have dementia. In the case of MAOIs, it's important to follow a strict diet, so these are not suitable for people with dementia. However, there is one MAOI called Manerix that does not have the same dietary restrictions, and there is some evidence to suggest that this drug may be useful in people with a decline in cognitive ability.

Restlessness, aggression and problem behaviour

As with depression, these symptoms can often be treated with social interaction, extra support and attention or psychological approaches designed to help calm the person. These might include music therapy (see p. 50) or reminiscence therapy (see p. 52). Treatment with medication should only be considered after these approaches have been tried, unless the person's behaviour becomes so problematic that it poses a risk to his own health and safety or that of his relatives or carers. If drug treatment is necessary, the doctor may prescribe antipsychotics (also known as tranquillizers or neuroleptics). These drugs can reduce aggression and, to a certain extent, psychotic symptoms such as hallucinations or delusions. Typically, they are given for a period of around three months, after which they can usually be stopped. There is no evidence to suggest that these drugs improve restlessness or other non-aggressive behavioural symptoms, nor that there is significant benefit in taking them for longer periods of time. The two drugs that appear to be most effective are risperidone, which may be sold with the brand name Risperdal, and aripiprazole (brand name Abilify). Side effects include dizziness, excessive sedation, unsteadiness, slowness, limb stiffness, chest infections, ankle swelling and falls. Antipsychotic drugs are particularly dangerous for people with Lewy body dementia, and should not be prescribed in these cases except with the utmost care, constant supervision and regular review by a doctor or consultant. See Chapter 6 for general advice on coping with difficult behaviour.

Non-drug treatments and therapies

As we have seen, the only anti-dementia drugs currently available are those used to treat the symptoms of Alzheimer's disease. These drugs don't work for everyone, and may only help in the early or middle stages of Alzheimer's. Even if your loved one is responding well to anti-dementia medication, there are a number of non-drug approaches that may help and can be used in conjunction with other treatments. It's best to talk to the GP or consultant about what therapies might be appropriate.

Aromatherapy

Aromatherapy is the use of fragrant essential oils to enhance psychological and physical well-being, and in particular to improve mood and promote relaxation. Oils can be added to bathwater, inhaled neat or added to water and heated in an oil burner to give off a pleasant fragrance. The use of oils is often combined with massage. Oils are diluted in a 'carrier oil' and then massaged into the skin. Lavender oil is well known for its relaxation and sleep-inducing qualities, and one study, which looked at the use of lavender oil on a hospital ward, indicated a reduction in agitated behaviour. Essential oils should be always used with care, after reading the instructions very carefully. It's best to check with a qualified aromatherapist before using them to help someone with dementia.

There is some evidence to suggest that aromatherapy, with or without massage, can help people with dementia to relax, and one study, which compared the benefits of aromatherapy and massage, aromatherapy and conversation, and massage only, found that the use of aromatherapy combined with massage could help to reduce wandering in people with dementia. There are some indications that aromatherapy may have a more significant role in treating Alzheimer's disease. Research funded by the Mental Health Foundation in 2000 suggested that lemon balm may help prevent the loss of the brain chemical acetylcholine. This suggests that lemon balm may work in the same way as the Alzheimer's drugs Aricept and Exelon. More research is needed.

Acupuncture

Acupuncture is a system of Chinese medicine that aims to stimulate the body's own healing responses by the use of fine needles inserted at strategic points around the body. Traditional Chinese philosophy teaches that health disorders arise from an imbalance in the flow of the body's natural energy, known as qi or chi. By inserting fine needles into the channels of energy, an acupuncturist can restore the balance, thus stimulating the body's healing process. Acupuncture grows ever more popular in the west, and some practitioners believe it reduces muscle tension and affects the way the body reacts to pain.

There have been a number of studies looking at the use of acupuncture as a complementary treatment for Alzheimer's and vascular dementia. These studies have all produced positive results, but the research is not considered to be of particularly good quality. Another small study, which looked at using acupuncture to treat anxiety and depression in dementia, found an improvement in these areas and also an apparent halt in mental decline. Experts say better-quality research is needed to confirm these encouraging findings. For more information on acupuncture, contact the British Medical Acupuncture Society (see Useful addresses).

Music therapy

This involves people with dementia playing instruments and making music with professional musicians who are trained in using music for therapeutic purposes. Studies have shown that music therapy can benefit many groups of people who are unable to communicate in the usual ways. For people with dementia, it is believed that music therapy may even slow down the progression of the disease. One idea is that, by stimulating the brain in this way, you are helping to keep brain connections working and making them less prone to degeneration. Whether or not it actually causes an improvement, it is clear that most people with dementia gain considerable enjoyment from the therapy. It has been shown that even people with very severe memory problems often remember the words and tunes of songs they know well, and singing along to these songs can prove a stimulating and enjoyable activity.

In terms of communication, music and sound may touch someone at a very deep level, providing comfort and tranquillity, or simply making the person feel happy. Therapy may take place in a group situation or on a one-to-one basis, with the musician playing music or sounds that the person enjoys for up to 30 minutes in a quiet room.

This type of therapy may include 'white noise', which is produced by combining different sound frequencies and can be used to drown out other sounds. White noise is sometimes combined with natural calming sounds such as birdsong, waves lapping on a beach or the sound of a babbling brook.

Research in care homes has shown that music or white noise therapy may benefit people with dementia. In one study, the treatment was used to help calm people who were frequently shouting. Another study found that when treatment with sedative medication was withdrawn and replaced by music therapy, there was no worsening of symptoms.

Bright light therapy

Many people with dementia experience increased restlessness and confusion around late afternoon and early evening. This has become known as 'sundowning', and may continue throughout the night. It is thought that it happens because of problems with the 'body clock' – the biological cycle of waking and sleep that is regulated by certain hormones, including melatonin, the 'sleepiness' hormone. During the hours of darkness the brain releases large amounts of melatonin to keep us asleep; when day breaks, light penetrates the brain via the retina causing melatonin production to cease and stimulating the release of 'waking' and activity hormones. If the brain does not receive enough light, the body clock is thrown off balance and the whole sleep pattern disrupted. Bright light therapy ensures that adequate light is delivered at the right time to help regulate the secretion of the sleep–wake hormones.

In people with dementia, increasing the levels of light may help to prevent 'sundowning' as well as disrupted sleep. The treatment involves the person sitting in front of a light box that delivers around 30 times more light than the average office light, for a set time each day, depending on individual needs and response to the treatment. Research has shown promising results for the effect the treatment has on restlessness and sleep disturbance in people with dementia.

Reminiscence therapy

Although people with dementia have difficulty making and storing new memories, they are often able to recall past events with surprising clarity. Reminiscence therapy is where people with dementia are encouraged to remember and talk about past experiences and events. This can be on a one-to-one basis or in a group setting, and is an activity that can be undertaken easily at home as well as in a day or residential care situation. Using prompts such as photographs, old magazines or newspapers, video recordings, music or other sound recordings may be helpful in getting the conversation going, and you might also like to introduce certain smells, tastes or textures. It may also be useful and enjoyable to put together a more permanent record in the form of a life-story book or a memory box (see p. 53).

There have been a number of studies looking at the potential benefits of reminiscence therapy, and while some of these suggest the therapy may improve cognition, recall and communication, and may help reduce low mood and depression, other studies have found little or no improvement. However, the activity is undoubtedly enjoyable, both for people with dementia and for their families and carers. It can also give family members, carers and care staff a deeper understanding of the person, making it easier to tailor the care specifically to suit that individual. Several studies carried out in care homes found that reminiscence therapy resulted in an increase in staff knowledge, which in turn increased motivation. Researchers have also noted a significant reduction in what they call 'caregiver strain'.

Reminiscing with someone who has dementia can be a rewarding experience for all the family, notably younger family members who may have found communication with their older relative difficult, especially following the onset of dementia. By interviewing the person with dementia about her life, and maybe even recording the conversation on video or audio tape or disc, loved ones will be able to see past the dementia and find a deeper connection with her, as well as gaining a valuable insight into family history. While it's fine to prompt your loved one if she gets a bit lost, remember that it's about what *she* remembers, so if she seems to be struggling, just move on and come back to that topic later. Bear in mind also that not all memories are happy ones, and she may become distressed if she remembers something sad or unpleasant. If she's upset, comfort her and allow her to talk about her feelings rather than changing the subject. She'll probably move on to a happier memory before too long.

Making a life-story book and a memory box

Helping your loved one to put together a life-story book and/ or a memory box can be an enjoyable activity for you both. It's something that can be added to over time, and even when there's nothing more to add it'll continue to provide stimulation and prompts to memory for discussion.

Life-story book

This is just like a scrap book, only more focused and with photographs. Start with an introduction, which may include a photograph of your loved one as a baby, a picture of the house she grew up in, her first school and the names of her friends. She, or you, can then write notes around the pictures: 'I was born on ...', 'My parents were called ...', 'We lived in ...', etc. As she builds her story, you might find certain headings will help her to remember and find appropriate photographs. Try headings like:

- my family, my friends (these headings might appear at several points throughout the book, as new family members are born and friends come and go)
- early years
- school days
- the world of work
- special days
- special places
- special things.

Don't rush the process – remembering her first job could lead to a long story about people she worked with, places she went to, achievements and disappointments. Let her reminisce, and don't be in a hurry to move on to the next topic. The book could take many, many hours to put together, but it will provide many more hours of pleasure, both in its creation and after.

Memory box

Use a storage box or an old shoebox. Decorate the outside to make it look special and then fill it with items that will act as memory prompts. These could be items with personal significance, such as medals, a wedding memento, an old tobacco tin, a letter or theatre ticket, or they could be more general things that will spark memories of an earlier time, for example old magazines or newspapers, food packaging and tins, cooking utensils, coronation or royal wedding china, and so on. Wartime items such as ration books and gas masks can prompt many a story. Again, you can add to the box over time. Ask friends and other family members to come up with items they think might be useful.

It may be a good idea to set aside a specific time each week for reminiscing with your loved one. You'll soon be able to judge the appropriate length of time to spend on the activity, but let her go at her own pace, and be sensitive to when she starts to tire or to lose interest.

6

Coping with the practicalities – memory and behaviour

When someone you love has dementia there are, as we have seen, many things to consider – legal matters, financial matters, how we talk about the condition, how we feel about what's happening, and so on. But when your relative is in the early stages of the illness, it's easy to push the practical, day-to-day problems that will inevitably arise eventually to the back of your mind. 'Okay,' you find yourself saying, 'so he's becoming more forgetful, but his memory's not that bad.' Or 'Yes, Mum repeats herself, but she hasn't started acting in a particularly strange or alarming way.' Or 'True, Dad was out in the garden rather late the other night but he hasn't started "wandering" – not as such.' The bottom line is: behaviour like this is likely to become a problem eventually, and if you can think about it and plan for before it starts to happen, it may be slightly – only slightly – more easy to deal with. If you have a loved one with dementia, think back to your old Boy Scout or Girl Guide days and remember the motto: 'Be prepared!'

Coping with memory loss

An increasingly poor memory is often one of the first noticeable symptoms of dementia. The odd lapse in memory is common as we age, but in someone with dementia the lapses will become more frequent, persistent and severe, even though there may be certain circumstances in which the person seems to have very good recall. When the forgetfulness starts to cause problems with daily life, it can become distressing, both for the person with the illness and those close to him. Problems your loved one may experience include:

- inability to retain new information
- forgetting names, or not recognizing friends and family
- general forgetfulness
- living in the past.

New information

People with dementia often find it difficult to take in and retain new information. This is because the part of the brain that processes new information may be damaged. So you may have a situation where, for example, you turn up to take your relative to the dentist, having told him that morning to be ready in an hour. He now swears blind you didn't tell him about the appointment. What has happened is that his brain was unable to process and store what you said, so for him it truly is as though you didn't tell him. When this starts to happen, it's a good idea to give him any new information in simple, 'bite-sized' chunks, and repeat it frequently.

Difficulty recognizing people

Your loved one may have difficulty remembering the names of people he has known for many years, or he may not recognize friends and neighbours. Eventually, he may not recognize close members of his family, or even his own reflection in the mirror. This is clearly upsetting for friends and relatives, who may feel rejected by the person with dementia. But it can also be distressing for the person concerned – he may think that relatives or visitors are intruders in his home, and this can be very frightening. Try to find ways to remind and reassure him. For example, rather than hoping he'll remember or asking if he knows who someone is, you could say something like 'Here's your youngest sister Jane come to see you.'

General forgetfulness

This can cause considerable difficulties in day-to-day life. He may forget where he's put something; he may go shopping and forget what he intended to buy; he may forget medical and other appointments; he may even forget to eat, or that he has eaten. In the earlier stages of dementia, memory aids such as Post-it notes, lists, timers or alarms and clear written instructions can all be useful. But as the condition progresses, the person may become confused about what these memory prompts are for.

Lynne's father was still driving in the early stages of his Alzheimer's disease, but his memory soon started to cause problems. As Lynne explains:

> One morning, he rang me to say that the car had been stolen from outside the house. By the time I got round there, he'd reported it to the police, and had even got on to the insurance people. Then we got a phone call from the police at midday to say they'd found the car. It was parked in the supermarket car park, where Dad had been shopping the day before, all locked up and with a long-expired pay-and-display ticket on the windscreen. Mum had seen him drive off the previous day, and just assumed he'd brought the car home again, although she did think he'd taken rather a long time to shop for the few things on the list. We think what must have happened is that he simply forgot that he had the car with him, possibly because he'd parked on one of the upper levels instead of his usual spot on the ground floor.
>
> After that, he used to take some sticky labels with the date on out with him. When he parked the car, he'd write the location on the label and attach it to his car key. That worked well for a few months, but it soon became clear that he would have to give up driving altogether.

(See p. 21 for more about driving and dementia.)

Living in the past

As we have seen, while people with dementia find it increasingly difficult to remember what happened yesterday or five minutes ago, their long-term memory often remains remarkably robust. They may remember things that happened 50 years ago with surprising clarity and detail. This can be interesting and entertaining for those around them, but may cause distress to the person in some circumstances. For example, if the memories are particularly vivid, the person may believe that he is actually living in an earlier time, maybe even as far back as childhood. He may insist, for example, that he has to get to school, or that his long-dead mother or grandpa will be coming to see him. If this happens, it's usually best to try to relate to what he is feeling, rather than to try and explain the reality.

Confusion

This is the term we often use to describe the sense of disorientation experienced by someone with dementia. As the condition progresses, the person with dementia finds herself feeling increasingly detached, and trapped in a reality with which she is not familiar. This is the result of problems with memory and communication, difficulties in relating to time and place, and changes in perception and understanding. Not surprisingly, this can be very frightening and distressing, and may significantly affect her mood and behaviour. She may become anxious or fearful, or may even become suspicious of the people around her, perhaps accusing them of stealing from her or of plotting to kill her.

For you, as relative, friend or carer, this can be terribly upsetting. There's the injustice of being seen as an enemy when you are devoting large amounts of time to helping her, but also there's wanting to comfort her, to explain the world to her and try to make it less frightening, and finding it virtually impossible because your world and hers are now two distinct and separate realities. Confusion is often worse when the person is feeling insecure or afraid. Try to be patient, and focus on what she might be feeling rather than what she actually says. So if she accuses you of stealing her handbag when in fact she has simply forgotten where she put it, don't waste time explaining that you didn't steal it: just help her to look for it and make sure she feels safe and reassured. Tell her that you will always help her to look for things if she can't find them.

Odd or unusual behaviour

The changes that cause someone with dementia to become confused can also be responsible for unusual behaviours that can be extremely irritating and time-consuming to deal with, but if you understand why your loved one is behaving in these often challenging ways you may find it slightly easier to stay calm and patient. Even if you do manage to stay calm, it's quite normal to feel upset, stressed and frustrated by your loved one's behaviour, and this can put a strain on your health and on your own relationships. It's very important that you address your own welfare as well as that of your relative, whether you are the main carer or play a more supportive role to the main carer. Have a look at Chapter 10, which addresses some of the difficulties involved in caring for someone with dementia and suggests ways of coping. Some of the most typical types of unusual behaviour include:

Repetitive speech and actions

Often, a person with dementia will repeat a phrase, question or action simply because he doesn't remember saying or doing it before. On the other hand, this type of behaviour may occur because he's bored, or because he's feeling anxious or insecure. If he asks the same question repeatedly, encourage him to try and find the answer for himself if possible. So if he wants to know what the time is or what's on television, remind him to look at his watch or to turn the television on. People with dementia often become anxious about forthcoming events, even if they are pleasurable, such as a visit to a relative or a trip to the seaside. Try not mentioning appointments, visits and trips until just before they're due to happen; this means there is less time to become anxious, and therefore less time for repeated questions.

If someone repeatedly asks to go home, it can mean that he's feeling anxious, insecure or unhappy. He may be in residential care or he may actually be in his own home, but asking to go home suggests that he doesn't feel as safe and secure as he used to. The concept of 'home' for him may evoke memories of an earlier time when he was comfortable in his own identity, and perhaps had the support and love of family members who are no longer around. Try to acknowledge his feelings, and reassure him that he is safe and loved.

Repetitive actions, such as moving things, packing and unpacking a bag or cupboard or making telephone calls, may relate to something the person used to do before he became ill, in terms of either employment or leisure. Use the action as an opportunity for discussion; ask him about his former job, hobbies or daily routines. Sometimes, repetitive actions or movements are simply a sign of boredom, in which case try and engage him in an activity or conversation and see whether this makes a difference. In some cases, repeated actions or movements can indicate discomfort. He may need to go to the toilet, he may be too hot or cold, or he may be hungry or thirsty. It's also possible that the movements may be a symptom of pain or illness, or may be a side effect of medication he's already taking. Contact the GP so these things can be checked.

Restlessness

Pacing up and down, fidgeting or generally being unable to settle is common in dementia. It may be because the person is uncomfortable in some way, so check to see whether she's hungry or thirsty, or whether she needs to use the loo. If she's pulling at her clothing it may be that it's too tight or that there's a label bothering her. If it's not caused by something external, you could try and distract her by giving her something to do with her hands. A box containing interesting objects might distract her, or she might feel reassured by having something to fiddle with, such as 'worry beads' or a soft toy. If she insists on pacing, make sure she wears comfortable shoes and check regularly for blisters, swelling or redness. Try and encourage her to rest every so often, perhaps by offering a drink or snack.

Night waking

Dementia can affect the 'body clock' – the natural 24-hour cycle that regulates our waking and sleeping. Your relative may get up at night, dress and even go outside. Obviously this can be both worrying and tiring for carers. Help him get a good night's sleep by making sure that he has enough exercise during the day and that he's used the toilet before bed. If he has trouble getting to sleep, a short walk, followed by milky drink and a warm bath with a few drops of lavender oil added, may help. If he gets up during the night, remind him that it is night-time and lead him gently back to bed.

Wandering

Like night waking, wandering in dementia can be a great worry for carers. It may occur for a number of reasons. It could be that the person simply forgot what she was doing; it may be that she has set off to search for someone or something from her past; it may be that she's unsettled by a change in surroundings, such as moving into residential care; or it may be that she has always enjoyed walking. If your relative wanders:

- try keeping a journal for a week or two to see if there's anything that triggers this behaviour;
- deter her from wandering by covering the exits with a curtain and keeping hats and coats out of sight;
- alert neighbours to the fact that she may wander;
- make sure she carries some easily spotted identification with contact details: for example, an identity bracelet or necklace;
- consider making the garden secure so that she can wander safely outdoors if necessary.

If she goes missing:

- search the house, garden, garage and shed or outbuildings;
- alert neighbours, and accept any offers of help to search for her;
- ask someone to stay in the house in case she returns;
- if you do not find her quickly, notify the police. Explain that she has dementia, and provide a recent photograph as well as a description of what she's wearing.

Bill's wife Sheila has vascular dementia. She had never 'wandered' as such, in that she'd never gone out of the house on her own, but she did go missing once while they were out Christmas shopping.

Sheila has always loved Christmas shopping. We'd spent the morning shopping for presents for the grandchildren and were just about to go and have some lunch, so I think the fact that she was tired and hungry may have had something to do with it. One minute she was standing next to me while I paid for the last purchase, then by the time I took my card out of the machine and looked around, she'd gone.

I didn't worry too much at first because I thought she couldn't have gone far, but she seemed to have vanished into thin air. I asked some of the shop assistants but they hadn't seen her, so then I went to the shopping centre security people, and they put out a message over the tannoy. I was sure someone would find her then, but still nothing. (It was only much later that I realized I'd got her description all wrong – I told them she was wearing a green anorak but in fact she was wearing a brown full-length coat!) The security staff were very kind, and eventually called the police for me. The police took it seriously because Sheila was classed as 'vulnerable'.

I didn't want to leave the shopping centre, but they said I should go home and wait in case she turned up there. In the end, she did come home on her own, but it was almost dark by then and I was worried sick. She'd been missing for nearly four hours. She was very upset and tearful, and she couldn't explain what had happened or where she'd been, but apart from that and being very tired, she was fine.

I went out the next day and bought her an identity bracelet and pendant, both of which I had engraved with the words: *I have dementia, please call* ... and there are three contact numbers. It's never happened since, but if it does, I feel happier knowing she has those contact numbers on her.

Following you around (trailing)

It can be very annoying when your relative with dementia follows you from room to room or calls out to you every couple of minutes to see where you are. But again it is probably due to the person feeling anxious and insecure. He needs to know that you are nearby in order to feel safe, and even if he saw you a minute ago, he may come looking for you again because he can't remember having seen you. To him, the minute may seem like several hours. If you have something that you can do within his line of vision, he'll feel reassured. But when this isn't possible, try to distract him with a task he can do alone or an activity he enjoys. Try not to speak sharply – this behaviour is incredibly irritating, but showing your frustration could make him even more anxious.

Hiding things

People with dementia often hide things for no apparent reason. They may then forget where the item is, or forget they've hidden it. Like so many of the odd behaviours seen in dementia, this can be the result of the person feeling detached and insecure. Taking something familiar and putting it in a secret place may stem from a desire to keep safe and hold on to things he feels he still understands. Try and identify favourite hiding places so that when he 'loses' something you can tactfully help him find it. If he's hiding food, check hiding places regularly, and discreetly dispose of anything that's in danger of becoming smelly! As always, even if his behaviour is driving you to distraction, try to be calm and reassuring.

Lack of inhibitions

People with dementia may behave in ways that are inappropriate or embarrassing for those around them. Often, this is because they have forgotten certain rules of etiquette or are just confused about what is appropriate behaviour. Sometimes, it may be because of damage to a specific part of the brain. This type of behaviour may include:

- Undressing in public – she may start taking her clothes off because she has forgotten that we usually undress at home, in private. She may be undressing because she's too hot or uncomfortable, because she's tired and wants to go to bed, or because she needs the loo. Gently guide her to somewhere private and try to find out what it is she needs.
- Inappropriate sexual behaviour – people who have dementia are still sexual beings, but the illness may damage the part of their brain that tells them what is appropriate in terms of sexual behaviour. They may make sexual advances to someone who is not their partner, or they may expose or touch themselves sexually in public. If this happens, try to discourage the behaviour by tactfully distracting your loved one's attention. Sometimes, the behaviour is not sexual at all, but simply appears so. When he touches his flies or she lifts her skirt, for example, it may simply indicate a need to go to the toilet.
- Behaving rudely towards others or being overly familiar with strangers – the person may swear, spit, say unpleasant things or insult people, or she may try to hug or kiss someone she doesn't even know. Again, the best thing to do is to try to distract her rather than attempt to correct the behaviour. Hopefully you'll have a chance to explain to the people concerned that it's the illness that's causing the behaviour.

Barbara is caring for her husband Jim at home. Jim was diagnosed with Alzheimer's disease three years ago.

> We're managing very well in general. Jim still does quite a lot around the house and in the garden, and he's still able to go for short walks

on his own as long as he has his phone with him. He's always been a sociable man and enjoys chatting to friends and neighbours, but the trouble is, he can no longer judge whether it's appropriate to talk to someone or not, so he talks to anyone as if he's known them all his life. Sometimes that isn't a problem, but it can be difficult if, for example, he approaches children in the park, or young girls on their way home from school. There was a time when he'd have realized that this could be misinterpreted, but he simply doesn't understand any more, and has sometimes been quite upset by people's reactions.

I mentioned the problem at the carers' group I attend locally (we meet every couple of weeks to discuss how things are going and share any tips). One of the women suggested making a badge for my husband to wear. I didn't like the idea at first – I thought it was literally 'labelling' him – but our daughter was all for it and Jim said he was quite happy to wear it, so that's what we've done. He now has a badge that says, 'My name is Jim. I have Alzheimer's disease, so please be patient!' It's actually made a huge difference locally, because not only are people not afraid of him any more, but they've been really kind. Once, someone even drove him home after he'd become a bit disorientated because of some road works. It may not be for everyone, but it's worth considering.

Shouting and screaming

Shouting or screaming may be the result of pain or illness, so this should always be checked first, because the dementia may make it impossible for your loved one to tell you what he's experiencing. Often, though, screaming or calling out stems from fear and/or confusion. It may be that he's having frightening hallucinations or other problems with visual perception – some people with dementia find heavily patterned carpets difficult to cope with, for example, because they can't see a simple pattern on a flat surface. If the screaming occurs at night, it could be that certain shadows or shapes look frightening in the dark. Try putting a nightlight in the room to reassure him. If he calls out for someone from his past, talk to him about this period of his life. This may be enough to settle him. He may call out in sheer despair if he's feeling afraid, distressed, lonely or bored, or if he's upset by too much noise and bustle going on around him. Try to establish what is causing him to feel unsettled. It may again just be a question of trying to reassure him.

General tips for coping with unusual or difficult behaviour

- All these behaviours can be annoying, embarrassing or both, but keep reminding yourself that your loved one isn't doing it deliberately.
- The behaviour is her way of communicating how she's feeling; if you can work out what she might be trying to express, it'll be easier to resolve the problem.
- Always reassure her that she is safe and loved. Try distracting her with calming activities, such as a hand massage, listening to music or stroking a pet.
- Try to ensure you have some support, and that you are able to take a break when you need to. Sometimes, if she's following you from room to room, for example, or saying the same thing over and over again, you may find her behaviour too much to bear, and worry that you will lose your temper. This is normal, but it's a sign that you need a break. If there is no one to take over, excuse yourself and leave the room for a while – even locking yourself in the loo for a few minutes can give you enough time to calm down.
- If you find the behaviour becomes impossible to deal with, talk to your GP. There may be some medication that might help, although this is usually considered a last-resort option.
- See Chapter 10 for more advice on coping with the difficulties of being a carer.

A dementia-friendly environment

Many of the difficulties experienced by people with dementia, such as confusion, anxiety, restlessness and even aggression, can be made worse by feelings of insecurity and the inability to make sense of their surroundings. The environment is important, and it's one thing that can be fairly easily changed to reduce its 'brain-scrambling' potential.

Background noise can increase confusion in someone with dementia, and can make him feel tired or even aggressive. Try to reduce unnecessary noise: so, for example, only have television on if he's watching it. Discourage children from all talking at the same time, and try to run noisy household appliances when he's in another room. Shopping centres or other noisy places can be very difficult for someone with dementia to cope with, especially as there's a lot of visual stimulation as well. It may be best to avoid shopping centres if you can, but if not, try to go at quieter times, walk where there aren't quite so many people, and consider getting him to wear earplugs if he finds the noise too much.

Avoid clutter, especially in kitchens or bathrooms where he has to concentrate on what he's doing. Remember that dementia can cause difficulty with coordination, so he may be more inclined to drop things or knock them over. It might help to decant things into plastic containers, where possible, and use unbreakable crockery. In the bathroom, buy shampoo and conditioner in one so there aren't too many bottles. Label taps, and try to make sure the hot water isn't too hot, just in case he forgets to add cold.

Try to remember that someone in the early stages of dementia will need help with organization, but will not ask for that help because he doesn't know he needs it! It's a question of trying to anticipate problems and then working out useful solutions. As the condition progresses, the person will need more and more help, but in the earlier stages it's better to try to find ways of offering support so that he can maintain his independence as much as possible.

7

Coping with the practicalities – the physical side

The previous chapter dealt more with difficulties surrounding memory loss, confusion and difficult behaviour. We know that dementia is a brain disorder, so we tend to focus on the psychological aspects of the disease. For this reason, and because communication inevitably becomes a problem for the person with dementia, the physical side of things may sometimes be overlooked. This chapter looks at the importance of maintaining health and fitness, common health problems, including problems with food and eating, and how to cope with incontinence.

Staying healthy

When people have dementia, staying fit and healthy is very important to help them get the most out of their lives. It's important that they continue to have regular health checks but they may forget to make appointments for the dentist, optician or chiropodist, so you may have to take over the arrangements yourself, or at least issue a few timely reminders! Encourage your relative to lead as healthy a lifestyle as possible in order to reduce the risk of developing other illnesses.

Exercise

Regular exercise will help keep your loved one physically and mentally healthy. Exercise should be something that can easily fit into the daily routine. Walking is ideal, whether it's a country hike, a walk to the shops or a stroll around the garden. The trick is to keep it manageable, so that it's well within her capabilities, and also to make sure it is regular. A five-minute walk every morning is of more benefit than an hour at the weekend. Gentle exercise will encourage her to stay mobile and maintain a level of independence. It also helps to prevent muscle stiffness or wasting, can reduce stress and anxiety and can help promote sleep. If your relative has reduced mobility, ask your GP or physiotherapist for some suggestions for exercise. There are a number of exercises that can be performed while sitting in a chair or wheelchair, or even while lying in bed.

Diet

We all know that a balanced diet helps to boost the immune system and increase our resistance to illness. But when someone has dementia, there can be problems with eating for a number of reasons, and this can lead to a poor diet with insufficient nutrients. (See p. 72.) In general, try to make sure that your relative is eating healthily. This simply means encouraging him to eat at least two pieces of fruit and three portions of vegetables each day. Bear in mind the 'rainbow' approach – fruit and vegetables in a variety of colours will ensure the best mix of vitamins and other nutrients. Keep processed foods, foods that are high in fat or salt, and sugary things like sweets, cakes and biscuits to a minimum, and encourage him to eat two portions of oily fish each week, as well as plenty of pulses, seeds and wholegrains. Wholemeal breads and high-fibre cereals, along with plenty of fruit and vegetables, will also help reduce the risk of constipation, which is common in older people and can cause a lot of pain and misery. Make sure he takes enough fluids each day, ideally eight cups or glasses a day. It's easy to forget to have a drink if you don't feel thirsty, and for someone with dementia it's even more likely. Not drinking enough fluids can lead to dehydration, which can cause tiredness, confusion, dizziness and fainting.

It's important not to neglect your own diet. Caring for or supporting a loved one with dementia can make huge demands on your energy. You may be so busy during the day that you only have time to grab a sandwich for lunch, then by the evening you're so tired that you end up getting a take-away rather than cooking. This is fine now and again, but if you neglect your diet for too long your health will suffer, even if it's just that you become more prone to picking up colds and viruses. Putting your loved one first doesn't mean you should put yourself last! See Chapter 10 for more about coping with being a carer.

Smoking

We all know how bad smoking is, but in someone with dementia, as well as being damaging to health, it can present a greater fire risk than in other people. Some people with dementia simply forget they smoke, especially if the cigarettes and ashtrays are removed from their sight, but someone who has smoked for many years may find it distressing and disorientating if she is no longer able to smoke. There is also an ethical issue – if adults have a right to smoke in their own homes, is it acceptable to prevent an adult with dementia from continuing to do something she has always done? This is a matter that should be discussed at an early stage if possible.

Alcohol

If someone is used to having a glass of wine with dinner, or a social drink at the weekend, there is no reason why this should change unless it becomes detrimental to his health or safety. In someone with dementia, problems can arise if he drinks more than he's used to because he forgets how many drinks he's had. Also, alcohol may not mix with some medications. If you're concerned about your relative's drinking, ask the GP for advice. A decision to stop someone from drinking alcohol should only be taken after weighing up the possible risks and balancing these against his rights to enjoy a drink as relaxation or as part of his social life.

Health problems in people with dementia

Dementia can make it difficult for the person who has it to recognize or report symptoms of health problems in the same way she used to. As the condition progresses, you will need to monitor your relative's health and watch for signs of pain, discomfort or low mood. If you help her to wash and dress, discreetly look for sore or reddened skin, rashes, blisters, corns or ingrown toenails. Any red patches that don't disappear within a few hours may be pressure sores. Tell your GP or nurse about this. Keep your eyes open for cuts and bruises as well – she may have fallen and forgotten to tell you about it.

Depression

Depression and low mood is very common in people with dementia. In the early stages, it can be a simple and understandable reaction to the diagnosis of dementia, or it may be due to chemical changes in the brain. If the depression is fairly mild, it may be possible to treat it with a programme of exercise or activity. But if it is more severe, your doctor may suggest a course of antidepressants. (See Chapter 5 for more about depression and how it is treated.)

Hearing problems

If your relative is unable to hear properly, it can add to his confusion and his sense of isolation. If you suspect he's having trouble hearing, ask the GP to refer her for a hearing test. In the meantime:

- Touch him gently on the arm when you are about to speak, and make sure you're facing him.
- Speak slowly and clearly, keep questions simple and only ask one question at a time.
- Reduce other noise – turn off the radio or television, and try to move away from any loud voices or noisy appliances.

Problems with eyesight

Like hearing difficulties, problems with eyesight can increase confusion in someone with dementia. It can make the dementia appear worse than it is because the person has difficulty recognizing people or being able to identify objects. If your relative appears to be having difficulty seeing clearly, arrange for her to have a sight test. On a daily basis, you might have to tactfully remind her to wear her glasses, make sure she has the right ones for reading and for distance, and make sure the lenses are clean.

Constipation

Constipation can cause severe pain and discomfort, and in someone with dementia it can also add to confusion. It's a common problem among elderly people, especially when they become less mobile. Prevention is always better then cure, so try to encourage your loved one to take regular exercise, drink plenty of fluids and eat plenty of high-fibre foods such as fruit and vegetables, wholemeal bread, cereals, beans and pulses. Eating a lot of fresh fruit may be difficult for some elderly people, so if he finds the idea of an apple or an orange a bit daunting, encourage him to take a couple of 'medicinal' spoonfuls of pureed prunes or apricots – even a small amount will help. If the problem persists, talk to your doctor or nurse.

Problems with eating

It is fairly common for people with dementia to develop problems with food and eating. Sometimes, they'll refuse to eat, pushing away the person trying to feed them, refusing to open their mouth, or turning their head away. At other times, they may accept food but then spit it out again, or just not swallow it. If this happens with your relative, try not to take it personally – she's not deliberately being difficult. It's more likely to be due to incorrect signals being received by the brain, or possibly to some discomfort in the mouth. It may be an idea to arrange a dental check-up, just to see whether there are any problems that may explain her reluctance to eat.

The Alzheimer's Society recommends three key principles when helping someone with dementia to eat:

- Keep calm – a calm, regular routine is reassuring for someone with dementia. Make mealtimes relaxed and unhurried occasions; turn off the radio or television and allow plenty of time for the meal. Never try to feed someone who is agitated, drowsy or lying down, as there is a danger of choking.
- Be flexible – eating habits are likely to change as the dementia progresses, so it helps to learn to accept that mealtimes may be very different to how they once were, or how you'd prefer them to be.
- Help the person to feel involved – if you have to feed your loved one, involve her in the process of eating: try putting food into her hand and guiding it to her mouth.

Weight loss and poor appetite

It is common for people in the later stages of dementia to lose weight for no apparent reason, and we don't yet know why this happens. However, weight loss as a result of poor appetite is also fairly common. There are a number of reasons why someone with dementia may lose interest in food or have a poor appetite. These include:

- Depression (see p. 44).
- Sore mouth or gums, badly fitting dentures.
- Constipation (see p. 70).
- Difficulties with chewing and swallowing – this can be a problem as dementia progresses. Ask your GP to put you in touch with a speech and language therapist, who may be able to offer useful advice.

In the later stages of dementia, the problems may be due to damage to the part of the brain that tells us what eating is for and how to do it. If the appropriate brain messages aren't getting through, the person may not understand why she needs to eat, even if she's hungry and even if her favourite food is on the table in front of her.

If your relative is still living alone, it may be that she's forgetting to eat her meals. This is an indication that she now needs a higher level of help. Try to arrange for someone to be with her at mealtimes to make sure she eats. Contact your local social services department to see if a home carer can come in and prepare a meal or just sit with her while she eats.

Weight gain and overeating

Again, overeating can occur because of damage to the brain, and it's often a temporary problem. On the other hand, it may have more to do with memory loss. In the same way that someone with dementia may forget to eat, it's also possible that he'll completely forget that he has eaten a meal. This can result in someone eating several extra meals a day, which as well as causing him to gain weight can also make him feel uncomfortable and overfull. If your relative is overeating, try to keep anything you don't want him to eat out of reach and sight. If you spot him attempting to eat when you know he's had sufficient food, try to distract him with an activity he enjoys. This may take his mind off food for a while. If you can't stop him from eating too much, try to make sure the food he eats is as healthy as possible. Foods like raw carrots, celery, peppers and so on are useful because they are healthy, low in calories. and will take time to eat. Fresh and dried fruit is also good, but bear in mind that fruit can be quite calorific, so if he's overweight carrot sticks might be a better option.

Helping your loved one to eat well

- Ensure she drinks enough fluids – she may not recognize the fact that she's thirsty – and that she eats a balanced and nutritious diet (see p. 68).
- If she's restless or has a poor appetite, she might find frequent small meals or snacks easier to cope with than three large meals a day.
- Check that food and drinks aren't too hot. She may lose the ability to judge temperature, or she may forget to check before drinking a cup of tea, for example.
- People with dementia often find that, due to changes in the brain, their tastes change as the illness progresses. They may want stronger flavoured and more highly seasoned foods than before. Just make sure they don't overuse seasonings like salt or chilli, as large quantities can be harmful.

Incontinence

Incontinence is very common in dementia, but it is not an inevitable consequence of the condition. Someone with dementia may become incontinent only on occasion, or it may happen most or all of the time. Whether it's an occasional or a regular occurrence, it can be distressing for everyone concerned, so it's a problem that needs to be addressed as soon as it becomes an issue.

Incontinence may be urinary or faecal. Urinary incontinence – an inability to control the bladder – is more common than faecal incontinence, which is an inability to control the bowels.

There are both medical and non-medical causes for incontinence. Medical causes include prostate trouble in men, urinary tract infections and severe constipation. Your doctor should be able to establish the cause and prescribe medication for any infection or, if the problem is with the prostate gland, he or she may recommend an operation. Constipation can put pressure on the bladder, leading to urinary incontinence, and can also cause faecal incontinence. The doctor may need to provide treatment if the constipation is very severe, but it's best to try and prevent the person from becoming constipated in the first place. See p. 70 for advice.

Non-medical causes include forgetting to go to the toilet or forgetting where to find it. Sometimes, because of damage to the brain, the person may not recognize the need to go to the toilet, or may become confused and use other items as a lavatory pan, such as a wastepaper or laundry basket.

Although some people with dementia are able to cope with the idea of incontinence better than others, many find it very distressing. It's common for the person to feel embarrassed or humiliated by what's happening. He may be upset that he needs someone else to help him with this very personal and intimate area of life. He may be particularly distressed at the thought of someone close to him being involved in this way. It is not uncommon for people with dementia to attempt to hide the fact that they've had an accident. They might take off wet or soiled clothes and try to hide them, or they may try to hide or parcel up their faeces so they can throw the package away.

Reducing the risk of accidents

Although you will need to acknowledge that there are bound to be accidents, there are ways of minimizing the risk:

- Ask him frequently whether he needs to go to the loo, and look for signs that he needs to go – fidgeting, for example, or pulling at his clothes. Lead him to the toilet if necessary.
- Try to establish a routine in terms of 'loo time'. This can help avoid faecal incontinence if his bowel movements are fairly regular.
- Make sure he knows where the toilet is, especially when he's in a different environment, such as visiting family or friends, or in a café or restaurant. It might be an idea to put a sign on the door –

a brightly coloured picture might be better than the word. Make sure the picture is at the right height for him to see it easily.

- Check that it's easy for him to get to the loo – are there any obstacles, such as awkwardly placed furniture? Are there any doors that are tricky to open? If it's very difficult for him to get to the toilet, a commode might be useful. Discuss this with your community nurse.
- Leave the door to the loo open so he can see that it's free.
- If necessary, adapt his clothing so that it's quicker to unfasten. Velcro fastenings may be better than zips or buttons, especially for people who have difficulty using their hands, perhaps because of arthritis or other health problems.
- Make sure he can get on and off the toilet easily – consider using a raised seat and installing handrails if this might help. Ask your GP to put you in touch with an occupational therapist who'll be able to advise you about this.
- If night wetting is a problem, encourage him to avoid drinks for the last couple of hours before bedtime. Don't restrict fluids during the day, though – this could cause him to become constipated or could lead to dehydration, both of which can increase confusion.

Practical aids

If incontinence becomes a more long-term problem, your doctor should be able to put you in touch with your local community nurse, continence advisor or occupational therapist. He or she can make a home visit to assess the situation, and can advise you on ways of making life easier and on taking practical steps to protect furniture, clothes and bedding. There are a number of items that may be helpful: some are available free from the community nurse or continence advisor, while others can be bought from the chemist. These include waterproof mattress covers, waterproof bedding, absorbent undersheets, and incontinence pants and pads.

What to do when your relative has an accident

It's important to approach continence problems in a matter-of-fact way. Although you know your relative can't help what's happening, it can sometimes be difficult not to feel angry or upset. If you show these feelings, she may become even more distressed and embarrassed. Try not to show your own embarrassment or distaste. It may be that approaching the situation with humour will make things easier for you both to cope with, but you need to be sure that this would be appropriate.

If she has an accident, help her to remove the wet or soiled clothing quickly. If her clothes are wet or soiled, not only will she feel uncomfortable but her skin could become sore or irritated as well. Help her to wash with a mild soap and warm water, and make sure she is properly dry before helping her into fresh clothes.

Tips for keeping odours at bay

- Wash wet clothes and bedding immediately or soak them in an airtight container until you can wash them.
- Use an appropriate container to dispose of used pads.
- Natural fibres are a good choice for clothing and bedding because they can be washed at higher temperatures.
- Keep a stock of moist toilet wipes for small accidents.
- Consider replacing items that seem to hold the odour.
- Experiment with deodorizing products until you find one that does the trick, but bear in mind that some strong-smelling disinfectants merely mask the odour. Bicarbonate of soda is a good natural deodorizer.

If you're finding it very difficult to cope with your own feelings about incontinence, try talking to a continence advisor or community nurse.

8

Outside help, benefits and services

Caring for someone with dementia can be time-consuming, expensive and exhausting, especially if you are the main carer, and especially in the later stages. You may cope well at first, and may not consider looking for outside help until you need it. But it's as well to be aware of what support is available so that you can access it quickly when you need to. There is a wide range of services available to people with dementia and their carers; these may be provided by the local authority, the NHS or by charities or voluntary organizations. When it comes to financial support, you and your loved one may be entitled to a number of different benefits, and you should claim these as soon as possible as they could make a significant difference to your daily life.

Claiming benefits

The benefits system is notoriously complicated for people with dementia and their carers. Some benefits depend on National Insurance contributions and some don't, some are taxable, others not, and some, but not all, are means-tested. Most benefits are paid through the Department of Work and Pensions. It is not practical to go into great detail here, but to give you a rough idea: at the very least, your loved one will probably be entitled to Attendance Allowance (AA) or the care component of Disability Living Allowance (DLA), and if you spend 35 hours or more a week looking after him, and the care component of his DLA is paid at the middle or higher rate, you may be entitled to Carer's Allowance. It doesn't matter whether you're related or whether you live at the same address, and you don't have to have paid National Insurance contributions to claim this benefit, but it is taxable, and you'll only be entitled to it if your earnings are below a certain level after allowable expenses. In some cases, Carer's Allowance may affect the benefits received by the person with dementia, so check this before you make a claim.

Other benefits that may be relevant include:

- Incapacity Benefit – this is payable to people under pension age who can't work because of illness or disability.
- Pension Credit – this is payable to people of 60 and over. It has two components: guarantee credit, which tops up a person's income to a set level, and savings credit, which is payable to people aged 65 and over who have income above the basic pension level, or who have savings or investments. Some people will be entitled to one part or the other, while others will be able to claim both parts.
- Housing Benefit – this is payable to people on a low income who have to pay rent and whose savings are below a set amount. It is assessed and paid by the local authority.
- Council Tax Benefit – some people may be entitled to a reduction in council tax if their income, savings and capital are below a certain level. Again, this is a local authority benefit.
- Income Support – payable to people aged 16–59 who are not working more than an average of 16 hours a week for reasons such as being a lone parent, being registered sick or disabled, or having to care for someone who is sick or elderly. You may not be able to claim if you have a partner who works for 24 hours a week or more, or if you have savings over a set amount.
- Winter Fuel Payments – people aged 60 or over should qualify for a payment to help with the cost of fuel. Those aged 80 or over may be able to claim a higher rate. For more information, call the Winter Fuel Payment helpline on 08459 15 15 15.
- NHS benefits such as free prescriptions and sight tests (which are automatically free for anyone aged 60 or over), vouchers towards the cost of glasses, free NHS dental treatment, free NHS appliances such as wigs and fabric supports, help with travel costs for NHS treatment.

This is by no means an exhaustive list, and some benefits may affect other benefits, so you really need expert advice on what you can claim. You can get advice on benefits from the Citizens Advice Bureau (CAB) or the Benefits Enquiry Line (see Useful addresses), who will be able to answer general queries and point you in the right direction for more detailed information. It may also be worth talking to your social worker, if you have one, or your local Alzheimer's society. The claim forms for some of these benefits are incredibly long and complicated, and you may be so reluctant to fill them in (I call this 'form-o-phobia') that you are put off making the claim. Don't be! Ask for help – there are many people out there who spend all day filling in forms like these and they'll be able to show you how to navigate your way through them. Talk to your social worker, your local CAB or your local Alzheimer's Society.

Collecting income from benefits – agents

These days most people have their benefits paid straight into a bank or building society account, but if your relative usually collects her benefit from the post office, it's a good idea for her to appoint you or another trusted friend or relative as her 'agent'. This involves informing the Department of Work and Pensions so that the benefit book can be issued in your name while you are acting as the person's 'authorized agent'. An authorized agent is able to collect benefit on behalf of the person with dementia. An agent can only be appointed by someone who is able to manage her money with support and who understands what appointing an agent involves. It is therefore a good idea to set this up while she is still able to manage her finances and make informed decisions.

Managing income from benefits – appointees

If your loved one is no longer able to manage her income from benefits, someone else may need to act on her behalf, administering her benefit income in her best interests and making sure all the appropriate benefits are claimed and all essentials are paid for. Someone who does this is called an 'appointee'. Wherever possible, this should be a close relative who lives with the person or at least visits very frequently. It is possible, in some cases, for a friend, neighbour or caring professional to become an appointee. If you wish to become an appointee, you'll need to contact your local Department of Work and Pensions and explain that your loved one has dementia and is no longer able to manage her benefits. They will ask you to complete a form, and then someone from their offices may visit her or ask for evidence to confirm that she is no longer able to manage her benefits. They'll also want to make sure that you understand the responsibilities you're taking on, and that you're a suitable person to be the appointee.

As the appointee, you'll need to:

- report any changes in her circumstances that may affect her benefit;
- sign on her behalf to allow the bank or building society to pay interest without deducting tax (if she's not a tax-payer);
- deal only with her income from benefits, except for very small amounts of savings that can be used for emergencies.

An appointee may resign if he or she is no longer able to act for the person with dementia. Usually, if someone else starts to act for the person under a lasting power of attorney (see p. 18) he will take over the appointee's duties. The Department of Work and Pensions has the power to revoke an appointeeship if there is evidence that the appointee is not acting in the best interests of the person with dementia.

Practical help

We all know that there's help available out there, but actually managing to access it can be challenging if you don't know where to start. Local authorities vary in what services they offer and in who provides them – some will be provided directly by the social services department, others may be arranged through other agencies or organizations. However, each local authority has a set of rules or eligibility criteria about what type of needs it will meet, and once someone with dementia has been assessed (see below) and his needs established, the local authority has a duty to provide those services that fall within the eligibility criteria. Most authorities will include services such as:

- Meals on wheels.
- Home care – this is where support is offered to help the person

with dementia remain in his own home. Again, services vary between local authorities, but the support should be tailored as much as possible to the person's needs. It may be as simple as one carer coming in for a few hours a week to help with shopping and housework, or it may involve a team of carers visiting throughout the day to help with personal care.

- Day care – many local authorities have day centres where people with dementia can socialize and take part in stimulating activities and therapies, as well as receiving personal care while they are at the centre. Transport to and from the centre is usually provided.
- Special equipment, e.g. memory aids, such as notice boards, special pill containers marked with the days of the week, or clocks with large faces; safety devices, such as gas detectors and water-level alerts; equipment to help with mobility, or with washing and using the toilet. It may also be possible to organize adaptations to the home if appropriate.
- Respite care (see p. 84).
- Care in a care home (see p. 90).

Community care assessment

This is an assessment of the person's care needs. It's carried out by the social services department and should be arranged as soon as it becomes clear that the person is confused or has dementia and needs support. You don't have to wait until the dementia has been formally diagnosed before asking for an assessment, and the local authority won't be able to arrange any support services until the assessment has been carried out. The assessment may include:

- a visit to the person with dementia to assess her health and disabilities, and to see what tasks she is able to cope with and what she may have difficulty with;
- talking to the person and her carer to ask about their needs and consider their views;
- identifying which of the person's needs the local authority is obliged to meet under its eligibility criteria;

- looking at the person's current living arrangements and discussing arrangements for future care;
- assessing the person's financial situation to establish what, if any, contribution she may be asked to make.

Carer's assessment

If you are, or soon will be, providing a substantial amount of care on a regular basis so that your loved one can stay in his own home, you will be entitled to a 'carer's assessment'. This is an assessment of your own needs, and it allows the local authority to provide you with services in your own right. It should take into account whether you participate or wish to participate in any work, education, training or leisure activity. This is based on the principle of equal opportunities – in other words, someone who is caring for a relative or friend should be able to take advantage of the same opportunities as someone who doesn't have caring responsibilities. If you haven't had a carer's assessment, ask the local authority to arrange one. When you're caring for someone with dementia, it's easy to push your own needs to the bottom of the priorities list. But it's very important for carers to maintain their own health and well-being, and the local authority can provide carers with support services. This may include short-term (respite) care for the person with dementia (see p. 84), although you may be asked to contribute to the cost of care.

Potential problems

Every local authority has its own criteria for eligibility, and the criteria may be set with that particular authority's resources in mind. If your request for assessment is turned down on the grounds that the person doesn't meet its criteria, it's worth writing to the authority to explain the circumstances in more detail, or asking someone else – perhaps someone from the Alzheimer's Society or the CAB – to write on your behalf. It's important to be persistent, and to make sure the authority has all the relevant information before making its decision. The local authority cannot refuse to assess someone on the grounds that the person's income or savings is sufficient to pay for his or her own care services.

The assessment

Assessments can be arranged though a GP referral, or by contacting social services directly. The person with dementia can do this himself, or you can do it on his behalf. The assessment may be completed in one visit, but if the person's needs are more complex it can be carried out over several weeks. The assessor will want to talk to the person with dementia and his main carers, and it's important that all those involved put their own point of view, even if opinions differ. It's a good idea to make some notes before the assessment, so that you can give the assessor a full picture of the situation, and also so that you can ask any relevant questions. In particular, write down details of the sort of care you're providing, of what you're finding difficult and of what might help make things easier (see the list on pp. 80–1).

The care plan

Once the person has been assessed, the social services department should produce a 'care plan'. This details the services that are to be provided, when they will be provided and by whom. You and your relative should be given a copy of the care plan (ask if you don't receive it). You should also be given the name of the person who is responsible for overseeing the plan and making sure it is put into practice. This person is usually called a 'care manager' and is the person with whom you should discuss any problems or questions you or your relative may have.

As your loved one's condition progresses, his needs are likely to change and therefore the services he receives may need to change as well. Social services will carry out reviews from time to time, but check with the care manager whether these will happen automatically or whether you need to arrange them yourself. But don't wait for a review if the services that are in place no longer meet the changing needs of the person with dementia: get in touch with the care manager as soon as possible.

Paying for services

In some cases services will be free, but the local authority is able to make a charge if, after assessing the person's financial situation, it decides that he is able to make a contribution to the cost of services it provides. Charges may vary between different authorities, but should always be 'reasonable'. If you or your relative think the charge is unreasonable, or if it would be difficult for him to meet, go back to social services and explain the situation. They may be able to reduce the charge. A service should not be stopped because the person is unable to pay.

Complaints

In some cases, people with dementia and their carers find they are 'doing battle' with local authorities. This can be very frustrating and upsetting, especially when there is so much else to think about at this time. Typically, problems include difficulty in arranging an assessment or having to wait ages for it to be carried out, difficulty in getting the local authority to agree to appropriate services, or long delays in getting them started after they have been agreed. Often, a few phone calls or a letter or email will do the trick – sometimes there is a breakdown in communication or things simply slip to the bottom of someone's 'to do' pile. But if this doesn't work, don't be afraid to make a complaint. There is a local authority complaints procedure (they can tell you how to use this), and if that doesn't work there are means of complaining at a higher level, for example to the Local Government Ombudsman Advice Team (see Useful addresses). You may also be able to get advice from a social worker, the CAB or the Alzheimer's Society. If you have a genuine complaint, don't be deterred from voicing it – and stand your ground!

Respite care

Respite care is a temporary arrangement for alternative care for the person with dementia. This is usually to give the regular carer a break, or because the regular carer needs time away for another reason. The carer may be ill or have to go into hospital, or it may be that he or she has other commitments – a family wedding, for example. Your relative will probably prefer to stay in her own home if that's practical, or it may be that a short stay in a residential care home is the best solution. If you're organizing respite care, consider whether you could get a relative or friend to take over for a while. If this isn't possible, there are a number of other options. If possible, you'll need to take into account your relative's own wishes regarding the respite period, her daily needs and the amount of money available to spend on respite care. You may be able to find a suitable home carer through the following:

- A home care agency – agencies can supply home carers to provide respite care, but these may be expensive. The local authority may have a list of home care agencies.
- The local authority – some local authorities may provide respite care at home.
- A carer who has been personally recommended – ask around among people you trust: your GP or community nurse, for example, other carers, or your local branch of the Alzheimer's Society.
- A 'care package' – this is the term often used to describe a 'team effort'. If your relative doesn't need 24-hour support, it may be that you can organize a care package involving friends, relatives, neighbours, social services, voluntary agencies and maybe some private care as well.

Finding the right person

- Interview the applicant yourself. Make sure the person has some experience or training in caring for someone with dementia. Always take up references.
- Be very clear about what the applicant's duties will be. So, for example, if they include some general housework or other task, such as walking the dog, make sure the applicant is happy with this. Check that he or she knows what these duties are and how often they should be carried out.
- Allow some time for the applicant to meet the person with dementia to make sure they get along and are both happy with the arrangements.

- Check the applicant's employment status – if he or she isn't self-employed, there could be a tax or national insurance issue. The Citizens Advice Bureau can advise you on this.

When you've found the right person

If possible, it's a good idea if the new carer can meet your relative two or three times before the period of respite care begins. This gives them a chance to get to know each other, and gives the temporary carer the opportunity to ask anything he or she isn't clear about. Whether these meetings happen or not, make sure you provide very clear instructions and explanations. These should include details of your loved one's usual daily routine – when he gets up, whether he likes to wash and dress straight away or whether he has breakfast first, whether he likes to go for a walk, etc. Make a note of any dietary requirements, including likes and dislikes. Be specific – instead of saying 'Tea at 11 a.m.,' say, 'Milky tea with one sugar at 11 a.m. He likes the yellow mug.'

Sometimes it can be difficult to remember all the things you (or another regular carer) know well and take for granted, so make notes for a couple of days to make sure that you don't miss anything, especially if your relative is in the later stages of dementia and has difficulty communicating. This could be very important in a situation where, for example, the person with dementia has a particular dislike – let's say he can't bear to have the television or radio on during the morning. The temporary carer may innocently put the radio on for a little music while preparing lunch. The person with dementia becomes upset, agitated and possibly difficult to look after, and it can take some time for the poor carer to realize what the problem is. It'll be time-consuming to note all these little details, but worth it in the long run, and of course you'll be able to use the same list for future periods of respite care. If your relative has made a life-story book (see p. 53) this will also be very useful for the temporary carer, and will provide a basis for conversation.

Don't forget to leave a list of important phone numbers (e.g. doctor's surgery) as well as contact details for other family members or friends who can be contacted in the event of any problems arising.

Temporary care away from home

This may be the most practical solution, but care away from home can be slightly more unsettling for the person with dementia simply because the surroundings will be unfamiliar, and she may be confused about why she has to stay somewhere else. Make it clear that the arrangement is temporary while you (or her main carer) have a rest, visit another relative, go into hospital or whatever the reason is. If she's upset, comfort her and reassure her that it's only for a short time, but stay calm and be firm – don't feel guilty for needing a break!

Visit the place beforehand, preferably with the person with dementia so that you can both be sure it's suitable and able to meet her needs. As with home care, it's a good idea to make staff aware of your loved one's preferred routine, likes and dislikes, etc. It will also help to pass on her life-story book if she has one, as this will help staff to understand and relate to her as an individual.

If she's fairly mobile and not too confused, a home providing residential care will probably suffice. Staff will usually provide help with washing, dressing and going to the loo, as well as support at mealtimes if needed. But if your relative is in the more advanced stages, if she's very confused, has difficulty moving around or has serious continence problems, you may need to find a home that provides nursing care. Homes providing nursing care may be more expensive than residential homes, but fees vary widely so it's an idea to look at several homes.

A community care assessment will establish the level of care needed. If your relative is assessed as needing and qualifying for short-term care, the local authority may provide it, although it may ask for a contribution towards the cost. It will assess the amount it thinks he can reasonably afford to pay by taking into account his income and capital. The amount should always be 'reasonable'. For someone who needs a high level of care, particularly in later stages of dementia, it may be possible for the NHS to provide short-term care. Ask your GP about this. There are no charges for NHS services, but any 'in-patient' stays may affect the person's benefits.

Before the respite care begins

Your loved one may be upset about you or another carer being away for a while, and if the respite care will be somewhere other than his own home, he may be particularly distressed because he doesn't understand what's happening. Try to minimize his distress, but don't feel guilty about it. It is not selfish to want some time to yourself, and you may even be putting your health at risk if you don't take the odd break.

Tips to avoid distress:

- Don't talk about the arrangements too far ahead of time (but don't leave it until the last minute, either!).
- When the time comes, refer to it as 'a little holiday' if the person will be staying away from home, or 'a nice change' if he's staying at home with a different carer. Talk about the respite period in a positive way.
- Reassure him that he'll be well looked after and that things will be back to normal very soon.
- Try not to show any anxiety or uncertainty you may feel about leaving him – if you're stressed, he'll pick it up. Stay calm, give him clear, straightforward answers to his questions, and reassure him without making too much fuss.

9

Permanent residential care

As we have seen, there are a great many services available to support people with dementia and to help them to continue to live independently. The most desirable option is usually to help people to stay in their own homes for as long as possible. However, as the condition progresses, there will come a time when this is no longer a practical or sensible option. This is usually when it becomes clear that, even with the support of family and professional carers, the person is no longer able to manage without some risk to health, safety and well-being. It may be that your loved one could move in with you or another relative for a while, but even this may have to be seen as a short-term solution, depending on the level of help and support she'll need. She may be upset at the suggestion of permanent care in a residential home, but you should not feel guilty for suggesting it. A good home will have staff trained in the care of people with dementia, and will be able to offer more specialized care than the most devoted friend or relative.

Who pays?

Having first arranged an up-to-date care assessment to establish the level of care required, your care manager will arrange for a financial assessment to be carried out. This will take into account income such as pensions, allowances such as Attendance Allowance and Disability Living Allowance, and income from investments or property, as well as looking at savings and capital. The assessor will use the whole picture to determine how much, if anything, your relative should contribute to the cost of residential care. If care is to be permanent, your relative's home may be taken into account, but not if his or her spouse continues to live there.

Choosing a care home

According to the Alzheimer's Society, two-thirds of care home residents in the UK have some form of dementia, so it's clearly a priority form of care for the care home sector. When choosing a home, the first thing you'll need to consider is whether your relative needs a residential or nursing home. This will depend on the level of care she needs. A residential home may be appropriate if she has difficulty managing to look after herself because of memory problems, but is still able to manage fairly well with a higher level of supervision and support than would be available at home. A nursing home has qualified nursing staff on duty 24 hours a day, and is more appropriate for those who need more focused nursing care, for example people who have had a stroke or other serious health problem such as severe heart failure, diabetes or arthritis. A nursing home may also be more appropriate for people with severe dementia, who have more complex physical and behavioural needs. Some residential homes have a nursing wing, so that if residents become more seriously ill while living there, they can simply be moved to the nursing wing rather than having to be moved into a hospital.

What to look for

When you start looking at the options for residential care, look at several homes and have high expectations. A good care home should offer 'person-centred' care. This means that staff should treat the person with dementia with dignity and respect at all times, which includes respecting the person's privacy; they should see her as an individual, and should focus on her personal qualities, abilities, interests, preferences and needs, rather than concentrating on her illness and its symptoms. They should aim to bring out the best in their residents with dementia, enriching their quality of life wherever possible. Ask to see the home's 'mission statement'. This is a written statement of the home's philosophy, and should make it easier to see how well the home is living up to its own standards. In many cases, you'll find the home's mission statement on its website.

All staff should be trained to understand the problems faced by people with dementia, particularly in terms of communication, and should be able to help them to express their needs. Even if your loved one is in the advanced stages of dementia, make sure staff are aware of how she prefers to be addressed – although many of us now quite happily use first names with doctors, solicitors and bank managers, many elderly people are still uncomfortable with this level of informality. Similarly, calling residents 'darling' or 'sweetheart' may be a genuine show of affection, but if your relative prefers to be addressed as 'Mr' or 'Mrs', ask the staff (nicely, of course!) to respect this.

You should expect the staff and care home manager to welcome you and be keen to answer any questions or concerns you may have. There should be at least one named member of staff who takes the main responsibility for each resident, although all staff should be able to interpret and meet his or her needs. The carer should have a clear picture of your loved one's life history, likes and dislikes, habits, preferences and special interests. A life-story book (see p. 53) can be useful here. A range of activities should be available so that there is something to suit everyone, and plenty of opportunities for socializing with other residents, as well as time to chat with staff. Visitors should be welcome at any reasonable time.

Some things to bear in mind when choosing a home:

- The location – how easy will it be for friends and relatives to visit?
- Does the home specialize in dementia care? If not, are staff adequately trained to meet the needs of someone with dementia?
- What are your first impressions? Is the place clean and well-kept? Is there a garden that residents can enjoy?
- What is the general atmosphere?
- Do residents seem happy and comfortable?
- Do staff seem cheerful and calm?
- Are they friendly and engaged with residents?
- Do they knock on residents' doors before entering?
- Are there enough staff on duty? There may be the odd staff shortage when various bugs are going around, but holidays and

longer periods of sickness should be covered, so being short-staffed should not be an ongoing problem.

- What are the rooms like? Are they comfortable and homely?
- Are there en-suite facilities, and if not, are there enough toilets and are they easy to get to?
- Can your loved one bring some possessions from home? Maybe a few small items of furniture?
- Is there a choice of meals? Ask to see sample menus. Will you be able to have the occasional meal with your relative? Try to check out the dining room at mealtimes. Are residents receiving help when they need it? Are they encouraged to eat and drink in a calm and friendly way?
- Is it possible for the partners of residents to sometimes stay overnight with their loved one should they wish to?

Of course, even the best-run homes can have the odd lapse – you may just happen to visit on a day when half the staff are off with the flu, half the residents have a tummy bug, the chef hasn't turned up and the pianist who was going to give an afternoon concert has fallen and broken his wrist. There is such a thing as a bad day! However, on a second visit it would be reasonable to expect many of these problems to have disappeared, so if the place is under-staffed and smelly, if the main meal is a fish-paste sandwich and the only entertainment on offer is a television that seems to be tuned to a channel to suit the carers, you may want to move to the next home on your list.

All care homes in the UK are inspected regularly by the Care Quality Commission (CQC) (see Useful addresses). Before making the final decision, have a look at the prospective home's recent inspection reports. These go into considerable detail about what the home does well, what it could improve on and whether there are any areas of concern.

What if your relative doesn't want to go?

Few people relish the idea of moving into residential care (although many are very happy once the move is made). One of the main fears is that of abandonment – your relative may be afraid that you have 'put him in a home' because you no longer love him or want to look after him. Reassure him that you do love him and that this is the best way for him to receive the specialized care he needs. Avoid statements like 'There's no other option' or 'I can't cope with looking after you any more'; instead, focus on the positive aspects – the activities, the opportunities for making new friends, the reassurance of having trained staff around 24 hours a day. It's a good idea to have done some preliminary research before raising the subject; that way, you can give your loved one a realistic idea of what to expect. Ideally, you could visit the home together, so you can take his views into account. It may be easier for him to adjust if he's been able to stay in the home for a trial period (see the section on respite care, p. 84) so try to arrange this if possible.

What if you have a complaint?

Unfortunately, even homes that appear well run at first can fall short of acceptable standards of care. Care staff, sometimes badly trained and often low-paid, may be overworked and 'too busy' to attend properly to residents' needs, leading to general physical and social neglect. In some cases, staff may be disrespectful, patronizing or rude, and at worst verbally, psychologically or physically abusive. People with dementia are vulnerable to all levels of abuse, and there have been some disturbing cases of severe ill-treatment in a small minority of homes. If you or other visitors have any concerns, do not be dissuaded from finding out what's going on. A care home that is doing its best to provide quality care will welcome the fact that you are drawing attention to any faults, and will see it as an opportunity to improve. If you do have concerns, you should first raise them with the care home manager.

In some circumstances, it may be that a constructive suggestion from you will resolve the problem – here is an example:

> Pauline's mum Dorothy had been fairly happy in her residential home for some months when Pauline noticed that her mum seemed a bit down and was losing weight, even though she would often have biscuits or cake with her tea. Pauline started visiting at mealtimes, and that's when she noticed that her mum was only eating small items she could pick up with her fingers – anything large, such as a portion of pie or a

large slice of meat, remained untouched. It transpired that the arthritis in Dorothy's hands had worsened, making it impossible for her to use an ordinary knife and fork.

Pauline spoke to the care supervisor about this, and the home immediately provided specially designed cutlery and allocated a member of staff to cut up food and make sure Dorothy was managing with her new knife and fork. Dorothy's mood improved (she had always enjoyed her food!) and she soon regained the lost weight.

If this is not appropriate in your case, and the outcome of your initial complaint is not satisfactory, ask for a copy of the home's complaints procedure – all homes are legally bound to have a simple, accessible complaints procedure. You can then decide whether to make a formal complaint. Complaints should be dealt with promptly, but at any rate within a maximum of 28 days, and as well as investigating the particular occasion you are complaining about, a good complaints procedure will also identify weaknesses so that action can be taken to prevent a similar thing from happening again. The home should keep a record of complaints, including details of investigations and action taken. This should be made available to the person making the complaint, as he or she may want to refer it directly to the Care Quality Commission (see Useful addresses).

In the majority of residential homes, staff caring for people with dementia are well-trained, committed to their jobs and determined to offer the highest possible standards of care. This should, of course, be the case in every care home.

Continuing the relationship when your relative is in residential care

It's very important to maintain relationships when someone moves into residential care, so when choosing a home you'll need to think about how often you'll be able to visit and the other options for contact. Is there a residents' telephone, for example? Stay in touch with other relatives and friends so that you can space out visits. It's usually better for your loved one to have frequent visits from one person at a time rather than the occasional visit from the whole family. When visiting, remember that this is now her home, so it's not like a hospital's 'visiting time' when you go in, sit by the bed, ask how the person is, eat her grapes and leave. It should be possible to spend a morning or even a whole day with your loved one. Take her out, if possible; have lunch together; join her for the afternoon's activities and meet her new friends. If you have been her main carer up until now, you may find your relationship becomes more relaxed and rewarding now that you are no longer responsible for her day-to-day needs.

10

Coping with being a carer

This is a topic big enough for a book in itself, and indeed there are some excellent books on the subject (see Further reading, p. 113) so I will not go into every aspect of caring and its joys and hardships in this limited space. Rather, I will attempt to give an overview of some of the aspects that seem to affect, to some degree, most people who are caring for someone with dementia.

You may be caring for your partner, a relative or in-law, or a dear friend or neighbour. You may have taken the role through choice, because you feel it's expected of you, because there's no one else to do it or because you feel it's your duty; you may find the experience rewarding and fulfilling, if tiring, or you may find it difficult and frustrating, especially if your relationship with the person you're caring for has always been problematic. Everyone's experience of caring is different, but for most people it's a bit of a mixture. There are some feelings common to all, and understanding the range of normal emotions can help you to get through what is likely to be a challenging time in your life.

How caring can affect you and your family

Much will depend on the level of responsibility you have. Does your role involve popping in every day to make sure your loved one hasn't forgotten to have lunch, or are you responsible for a higher level of care, including personal care such as helping with feeding, washing and dressing? Even if the amount of time you spend physically helping your loved one is relatively small, you may still feel overwhelmed by having to plan, organize and remember everything for two.

Are you the sole carer, or is the responsibility shared between you and other family friends or relatives? If it seems you have an unfair share of the workload, you are likely to feel anger and resentment towards other family members, or possibly towards the person with dementia. The first thing you need to do is to establish why you're doing so much of the work. Could it be that others simply don't realize how much work is involved in caring for someone with dementia? It may be that they're reluctant to offer help in case you think they're 'interfering' or are suggesting you can't cope. It may be that they see you getting on with it and assume everything's fine. In a few cases, they know it's tough, they know you're having trouble coping, but they're just ignoring the problem. Whatever the situation in your own case, if you're feeling resentful, tired, frustrated or taken advantage of, you need to address these feelings and talk to the other people involved, because the situation won't get better without some action being taken.

It's always a good idea to have a family conference soon after dementia is diagnosed. That way, plans can be made in advance, with the person's own input into how he or she would prefer to be cared for. But even when plans have been made for sharing the workload, these plans may not be adhered to when the situation becomes a reality. Or it may be that the level of care increases, so that what was fine and easy to cope with at the start gradually becomes too much for one person.

In some cases, relatives make unfair assumptions about who should undertake the bulk of the caring. Traditionally, 'caring' is seen as being a woman's role, something that women are naturally designed and emotionally equipped to do. A single woman is likely to find herself the 'obvious' choice as main carer; after all, what else does she have to do with her life? These assumptions must be challenged, even if it leads to conflict within your family. If your relative needs help for, say, 20 hours a week, there is no reason why it is more appropriate for a single woman to give up her job and social life to provide it than her married brother. It should be possible to split the care. It may not be possible to do ten hours each, every week. But it should be possible to come to an arrangement that helps everyone to maintain at least some of their working and social life, even if that means they have to work part-time or give up a few nights out.

You may, of course, choose to give up your job to take the role of a full-time carer, but this still doesn't mean you should have sole responsibility for the person you are caring for. You will need breaks, short ones and longer ones. You will possibly need them more than someone with a high-powered career. Never underestimate the value of what you're doing, and the toll it can take on your physical and emotional health. In terms of getting the rest of the family – and indeed, social services – to take note, the key is to have open and frank discussions. If you don't speak up, everyone will assume you're coping.

Loss and grief

Sadly, as dementia progresses the person's identity is gradually eroded, and you're likely to feel a strong sense of loss and grief for the individual you knew and loved. Because of the nature of the illness, it's like a series of small losses; just as you come to terms with one stage of the person's illness, you find that his abilities decline further and his behaviour changes once more, and then you grieve all over again. Depending on the nature of your relationship with the person, you may feel a sense of loss for the future you'd planned together and for the companionship you shared. You may also grieve for your job, for financial security or for your previous lifestyle. For loved ones, it's like a premature bereavement, with the added difficulty that you cannot take time away to gradually recover from your loss, because you still have to look after the person on a daily basis, all the time feeling that you just want your loved one back. Allow yourself to feel sad; it is a sad situation.

Your other relationships

If you're spending a great deal of time caring for a relative or friend with dementia, it can impact on your own personal relationships. Your partner may feel neglected and resentful, or may even be angry with you for spending so much time and energy on the other person's well-being. There is no easy solution to this problem, but you can help matters a great deal by simply talking about the issues with your partner. If you meet your partner's objections with a defensive statement or a raised voice, the whole thing is likely to spiral out of control.

Try to talk about it when you're both feeling calm and relaxed, rather than when you've just got in from a gruelling day. Be honest about how you feel, and encourage your partner to be honest as well. Try to avoid negative statements, so instead of saying, 'I wish you wouldn't keep going on about me spending so much time at Mum's,' try something like, 'I really wish I could spend more time with you – I miss being at home with you in the evenings – but at the moment, my mum needs my help.'

It may help your partner to understand if you gently raise the topic of his or her own parents. Don't yell, 'How would you feel if it was *your* mother?' Rather, perhaps say something like, 'I really hope your mum never needs the level of care my mum does, but should that happen, I hope I'd be able to understand and support you in caring for her.' It can also help to share feelings with your partner: 'Yes, I feel angry and resentful about it too. I'm so glad I can talk to you about it.'

Don't let problems in your relationship get out of hand. If necessary, contact Relate (see Useful addresses). Relate counsellors have plenty of experience in helping couples who are going through a difficult time in their lives.

Caring and your own health

It is estimated that, at any one time, up to two-thirds of carers suffer from depression (see p. 46 for signs and symptoms of depression). Your physical health can suffer too – sheer exhaustion, worry and poor eating habits can knock your immune system for six and make you vulnerable to infection. Lifting someone in and out of bed can damage your back, and stress can cause headaches, insomnia, stomach trouble and skin problems.

It is often said that people who are caring for someone with dementia may suffer a similar type of stress to that experienced by parents of young children. This may be because some of the behaviours found in Alzheimer's and other dementias are similar to those that parents find most challenging in children, i.e. night waking, incontinence, constant questioning, constant following around (trailing). In the same way that new parents often find comfort and moral support in talking to other new parents, you may find it helps to talk to other people who are caring for someone with dementia. Your local Alzheimer's society will be able to point you to local carers' groups, and they also have a helpline which you can call for information or simply to talk to someone if you're having a bad day: Dementia Helpline 0845 300 0336. You may also find it useful to join one or more of the many online forums for carers. The Alzheimer's Society has its own forum at <www.alzheimers.org. uk/talkingpoint>. It's also worth contacting Carers UK (see Useful addresses).

If your physical health is suffering or you think you may be depressed, don't ignore it. See your GP as soon as possible so that the problem can be diagnosed and treated. Looking after your own mind and body is far from selfish – you won't be able to carry out your caring work if you're ill. This may also be a good time to organize some respite care so that you can have a break, either to give you time to recover from existing health problems or simply to recharge your batteries so that you don't become ill.

Coping with the later stages

In the later stages of dementia, your relative may start to display more of the unusual behaviours mentioned in Chapter 6. This can be where it becomes particularly challenging for family and friends. As has been mentioned throughout the book, the only way to try to deal with these behaviours is to remember that it is coming from the illness, not the person. It can be very distressing when, for example, your loved one doesn't recognize you. This is not simply a question of forgetting a name, but seems to arise from damage to particular areas of the brain that control recognition. In extreme cases, the person with dementia may believe that a loved one has been replaced by an impostor. This can be very distressing, both for the person accused of being an impostor and for the person with dementia. In some cases, the person fails to recognize his home, and may be convinced that he has two houses and needs to get back to the other one. If this happens, try taking him out for a short walk or ride in a car or bus, then simply coming back to the same house. Often, he'll be satisfied on his return that he's now in the right house.

It's fairly common for people in the later stages of dementia to forget major events in their lives, such as the death of a spouse or parent. There is then a dilemma for other relatives and carers – do they correct the person or not? It's difficult to know what to do in this situation, but try to decide how best to minimize distress. So if, for example, your 98-year-old dad mentions his parents as if they are still alive, it may be best to go along with it. If he wants to see them, you could try saying he can see them later. But if he repeatedly asks to visit them and is upset by not being able to, you may have to remind him that they are dead. Unfortunately, if he doesn't remember their deaths, he may experience bereavement all over again.

Communication becomes more difficult in the later stages. Your loved one may be unable to speak or to demonstrate that she knows you're there, but talking softly to her, stroking her hand or just linking your arm through hers may offer her some comfort and reassurance. It may also be comforting for you.

Jackie's mother-in-law died recently, having been in residential care for a total of five years. For the last few months of her life, Nellie was unable to communicate in the usual ways, but Jackie discovered a novel way of relating to her mum-in law, and now has fond memories of those last months.

I used to visit Nellie once a week. About six months before she died, I'd started to wonder whether there was any point in visiting her. She didn't know who I was and didn't even seem to register that anyone was there at all, but I used to sit with her and just talk about the family and what had been going on. One day, I knocked over a glass of water, and automatically swore. Nellie laughed. I hadn't heard her make a sound for weeks, so it was quite something. One of the carers was in the room at the time, and she said, 'Oh, I see, Nellie. Takes a naughty word to get you laughing, does it?' She was just being cheerful, and went out of the room as soon as she'd finished what she was doing, but it made me wonder, so I thought I'd just try it. I leaned closer to Nellie, and said the word again. Again she laughed. I tried another swear word, and she laughed again! By the end of my visit, Nellie and I were both giggling like schoolgirls. It tickled me because before she was ill Nellie was always rather prim and proper.

Anyway, I thought it was just a one-off, but the next time I visited I thought I'd just give it another go. Sure enough, she started chuckling away as soon as I said something rude. It became something we'd do together every week. We'd just laugh and laugh and laugh. I started really enjoying those visits. I don't know how much Nellie understood, but the carers said she was always a little calmer and easier to deal with on those days. When I told my brother-in-law (Nellie's son), he was appalled. He said it was taking away her dignity. Maybe he was right, but all I know is, she seemed to take absolute delight in those little sessions, and the carers actually commented on how my visits cheered her up – I'd been visiting her on my own for two years, ever since my husband died, and they never said anything before. I can't see the harm.

My advice to anyone else would be: do whatever it takes to build some communication between you. A neighbour of mine has a husband with advanced dementia, and she says she just talks gibberish to him, but he responds in a way that he doesn't to normal conversation, so what's the harm?

Another problem for carers of someone in the later stages of dementia is coping with aggression. If your loved one becomes aggressive, the most important thing is to keep yourself safe. It's important to remember that it's the illness that is making her behave in this way, but that doesn't mean you must put up with being punched or hit or pushed around. Try to anticipate when she's likely to become aggressive; take note of anything that seems to trigger this sort of behaviour, and remove yourself from the situation until she calms down again. Ultimately, it may be that medication is needed.

The advanced stages of dementia are particularly difficult to cope with because it's almost as though the person you are caring for is a stranger. Given the sheer amount of work and stress involved, it's hard enough to cope when your relative is being sweet and charming and is still recognizable as the person you've loved for many years, possibly all your life. But when that person seems to have been replaced by an unpleasant stranger who is constantly hostile towards you and seems hell-bent on making your life a misery, it can be difficult not to just turn and run away. And then you feel guilty for thinking such a thing ...

Guilt

Guilt is one of the most common emotions felt by carers. You may feel guilty for many reasons:

- You find yourself feeling angry or irritated with your loved one for forgetting something, and you know she can't help it, so you feel guilty.
- Sometimes she does remember things, and you start to think she *can* help it, then you feel guilty about thinking that.
- You feel you've been forced into a caring role, and you feel guilty for feeling resentful.
- You're happy to care for your loved one, but feel guilty because you don't do more and spend more time with her. Other carers seem to do so much more.
- You do as much as you're physically able, and you spend lots of time just keeping her company. But you feel you're neglecting your partner, so you feel guilty for that.
- You've cared for your loved one for years, and now her dementia is so advanced that she needs more care than you are able to provide. You make the decision to look into residential care, and feel guilty.
- You're run down and exhausted, and not surprisingly you've succumbed to flu. You have a raging fever and can barely lift your head from the pillow. You're very ill. And yet you still feel guilty . . .

The point I'm making is that the guilt felt by carers is very rarely justified: it's just another emotion to drain you yet further. One of the best ways of dealing with negative emotions such as guilt, frustration or anger is to talk about how you feel, whether to a friend or relative, an understanding professional, a counsellor or to other people who understand what you're going through. You need to acknowledge your feelings rather than bottling them up. Try to work out why you're feeling guilty, and be aware of what effect these feelings are having on you. For example, are you pushing yourself too hard to compensate for things you feel guilty about?

The Alzheimer's Society can offer emotional as well as practical support to carers of people with Alzheimer's or other dementias.

They can put you in touch with carers' groups in your area, and also run an online forum if you prefer more anonymous contact. The forum can be found at <www.alzheimers.org.uk/talkingpoint>.

There is a lot of support out there, but you need to ask for it. Although we tend not to want to be labelled, thinking of yourself as a 'carer' rather than who you really are (wife, husband, partner, daughter, son, sibling, friend) will help you to access the support you need. There are a number or organizations that can help, in particular the Alzheimer's Society and Carers UK (see Useful addresses). There are also useful books on the subject (see Further reading), in particular *The 36-Hour Day: A Family Guide for Carers of Persons with Alzheimer's Disease, Related Dementing Illnesses and Memory Loss in Later Life*. The first part of the title sums it up, really.

To cope successfully with caring, you need to look after yourself. Take regular breaks away from the person you are caring for, and don't feel guilty about it. Make time for yourself: time to relax, time to think, time to socialize with friends and family, time to pursue your own hobbies or interests. Taking care of yourself will help you to cope better with caring, and to enjoy a better relationship with the person with dementia, as well as with your other family and friends. Most carers agree that, despite the gruelling hours of work, the challenges and the tears, caring can bring enormous rewards and a great deal of joy and laughter. Make sure you're strong enough to cope with the downside, and well enough to enjoy the ups!

The final stages

When your loved one reaches the final stages of dementia, he may be unable to recognize or communicate with you. In many ways, it is as though he has already gone, and yet you cannot mourn him properly because he is still alive. When verbal or visual communication is no longer possible, it may be comforting for both of you if you sit with him and hold or stroke his hand. Recognize that you have done all you could do, and be prepared for the difficult feelings you may experience after he dies.

Some people find that they have grieved so much throughout their loved one's illness that they don't experience any strong feelings after the person dies. This is very common and perfectly understandable, so don't feel bad about not having a reaction – you *have* reacted. Others go though a range of emotions in the period after the person's death, including:

- disbelief, denial;
- anger and resentment;
- relief, both for themselves, and for the person with dementia;
- guilt;
- sadness and pain;
- shock – even if the death has been expected for some time.

In addition to these emotions, someone who has been a full-time (or mostly full-time) carer is likely to feel a lack of purpose and a sense of emptiness after the person with dementia dies. Even if you haven't been a full-time carer, or the person has been in residential care, you may still feel a void in your life. It can take a long time to come to terms with the person's death, and you'll need the support of your family and friends during this difficult period. It may also help to talk to the Alzheimer's Society, Carers UK or *for dementia* (Admiral Nurses), or try a bereavement support service such as Cruse Bereavement Care (see Useful addresses).

Give yourself time to recover. Accept that you may feel tired and perhaps a little bewildered for a while. You may feel better for a few days, only to suddenly find yourself overcome with sadness again. Bereaved people often find the first year very difficult – the first birthday, Christmas, anniversaries. You may need extra support at this time.

In time, you will pick up the threads of your life; you'll find that you are able to talk about your loved one again, and to reminisce and share memories with friends and family. And if you devoted time to care for that person, even if it was only for a few hours a week or as part of a big team of carers, just remember that you will have done a great deal to make his or her life more comfortable and secure in those final years.

Appendix
People you may encounter

You're likely to come into contact with a number of healthcare professionals who have various roles to play in the care and treatment of someone with dementia. Many of these people will work together, as part of a 'healthcare team'. These may include:

- Your GP – looks after general health matters and is the first point of contact. The GP can make referrals to other healthcare professionals, such as a consultant.
- Consultant – consultants are doctors who have extensive training, qualifications and experience in a particular speciality. Someone with dementia may encounter a consultant neurologist, who specializes in disorders of the brain and nervous system; a geriatrician, who specializes in the physical health of older people; a psychiatrist, who specializes in mental health problems; or a geropsychiatrist, who has had further training in the mental health problems of older people.
- District or community nurse – has had extra training so that he or she is able to nurse people at home.
- Community mental health nurse (also called community psychiatric nurse or CPN) – provides treatment, care and support to people with mental health problems and dementia. A CPN can carry out assessments and advise people with dementia and their carers on ways of coping and improving their quality of life. Your GP or consultant will be able to refer you to a CPN.
- Social workers (sometimes called 'care managers') – assess the person's needs with regard to care and services, and will also be involved in planning and co-ordinating the delivery of those services. They can also offer support to people with dementia and their carers.
- Care workers (also known as care attendants) – may work with the person at home or in a residential care setting. They usually help with personal care: getting the person washed and dressed,

for example, changing bedding and doing laundry, helping at mealtimes and putting the person to bed.

- Continence advisor – offers advice on incontinence, including information on equipment such as pads, waterproof bedding and commodes. Ask your GP to refer you.
- Clinical psychologists – often work with consultants in memory clinics. They assess memory, learning ability and other skills, and can offer support.
- Occupational therapist (OT) – can advise on special equipment and home adaptations that can make life easier for people with dementia and help them to maintain their independence for longer. If you think an OT may be useful, ask your GP, consultant or social worker.
- Physiotherapist – can advise on maintaining mobility as dementia progresses. Sessions may take place in hospital, at a community clinic or in the person's own home. Your GP or consultant can make a referral.
- Speech and language therapist – can help people with dementia and their carers to communicate more effectively. Can also help with eating and swallowing difficulties. Ask your GP for a referral.
- Admiral nurses – specialist dementia nurses supported by the charity *for dementia* (see Useful addresses). They provide practical, emotional and personal support to people with dementia and their families and carers, including professional carers. Support lasts as long as it is required, from first contract to post-bereavement. This service is not currently available countrywide, but is expanding rapidly. If it hasn't reached your area yet, you may find the Admiral Nursing DIRECT helpline useful: 0845 257 9406. At the time of writing, the helpline is only operating on Tuesdays and Thursdays from 11 a.m. to 9 p.m. It is hoped this will soon be extended. You can leave a message outside of these hours and an Admiral nurse will get back to you.

Useful addresses

Admiral Nursing DIRECT
Helpline: 0845 257 9406 (currently 11 a.m.–9 p.m., Tuesday and Thursday only; leave a message outside of these hours)

Age Concern Cymru (Wales)
Ty John Pathy
13–14 Neptune Court
Vanguard Way
Cardiff CF24 5PJ
Tel.: 029 2043 1555
Website: www.accymru.org.uk

The four national Age Concerns in the UK have joined together with Help the Aged. For local branch details, visit the website or telephone the head office.

Age Concern England
Astral House
1268 London Road
London SW16 4ER
Tel.: 020 8765 7200
Free helpline: 0800 009966 (8 a.m.–7 p.m., seven days a week)
Website: www.ageconcern.org.uk

Age Concern Northern Ireland
3 Lower Crescent
Belfast BT7 1NR
Tel.: 028 9024 5729
Website: www.ageconcernni.org

Age Concern Scotland
Causewayside House
160 Causewayside
Edinburgh EH9 1PR
Tel.: 0845 833 0200
Website: www.ageconcernandhelptheagedscotland.org.uk

Alzheimer Scotland
22 Drumsheugh Gardens
Edinburgh EH3 7RN
Tel.: 0131 243 1453
Freephone 24-hour Dementia Helpline: 0808 808 3000
Website: www.alzscot.org

Alzheimer's Society
Devon House
58 St Katharine's Way
London E1W 1JX
Tel.: 020 7423 3500
Dementia Helpline: 0845 300 0336 (8.30 a.m.–6.30 p.m., Monday to Friday)
Website: www.alzheimers.org.uk

For local branch contact details, look on the website or telephone the head office.

Benefit Enquiry Line
Freephone: 0800 882 200 (8.30 a.m.–6.30 p.m., Monday to Friday; 9 a.m.–1 p.m., Saturday)

Bladder and Bowel Foundation
SATRA Innovation Park
Rockingham Road
Kettering NN16 9JH
Tel. (general enquiries): 01536 533255
Nurse helpline for medical advice: 0845 345 0165
Counsellor helpline: 0870 770 3246
Website: www.bladderandbowelfoundation.org

British Association for Counselling and Psychotherapy
BACP House
15 St John's Business Park
Lutterworth LE17 4HB
Tel.: 01455 883300
Website: www.bacp.co.uk

British Medical Acupuncture Society
BMAS House
3 Winnington Court
Northwich
Cheshire CW8 1AQ
Tel.: 01606 786782
Website: www.medical-acupuncture.co.uk

There is also a London office (for contact details see the website).

Care Quality Commission
National Correspondance
Citygate
Gallowgate
Newcastle upon Tyne NE1 4PA
Tel.: 03000 616161
Website: www.cqc.org.uk

Provides access to inspection reports on residential care homes.

Carers Northern Ireland
58 Howard Street
Belfast BT1 6PJ
Tel.: 028 9043 9843
Website: www.carersni.org

Carers Scotland
The Cottage
21 Pearce Street
Glasgow G51 3UT
Tel.: 0141 445 3070
Website: www.carerscotland.org

Carers UK
20 Great Dover Street
London SE1 4LX
Tel.: 020 7378 4999
CarersLine: 0808 808 7777 (10 a.m.–midday and 2–4 p.m., Wednesday
and Thursday)
Website: www.carersuk.org

Carers Wales
River House
Ynsbridge Court
Gwaelod-y-Garth
Cardiff CF15 9SS
Tel.: 029 2081 1370
Website: www.carerswales.org

Citizens Advice
Tel.: 020 7833 2181 (admin only; no advice available on this number)
Website: www.citizensadvice.org.uk

See the website for details of your local Citizens Advice Bureau.

Counsel and Care
Twyman House
16 Bonny Street
London NW1 9PG
Tel.: 020 7241 8555
Advice line: 0845 300 7585 (10 a.m.–4 p.m., Monday, Tuesday, Thursday
and Friday; 10 a.m.–1 p.m., Wednesday)
Website: www.counselandcare.org.uk

Offers support and advice for older people, their families and carers.

Crossroads Association
10 Regent Place
Rugby
Warwickshire CV21 2PN
Tel.: 0845 450 0350
Website: www.crossroads.org.uk

Charity offering support for carers.

Cruse Bereavement Care
PO Box 800
Richmond
Surrey TW9 1RG
Day by Day Helpline: 0844 477 9400
Website: www.crusebereavementcare.org.uk

Dementia Advocacy and Support Network International
PO Box 1645
Mariposa
California
USA 95338
Website: www.dasninternational.org

for dementia
6 Camden High Street
London NW1 0JH
Tel.: 020 7874 7210
Website: www.fordementia.org.uk

Supports Admiral nurses; see also Admiral Nursing DIRECT.

Local Government Ombudsman
PO Box 4771
Coventry CV4 0EH
Advice line: 0845 602 1983 or 0300 061 0614
Website: www.lgo.org.uk

MIND (National Association for Mental Health)
15–19 Broadway
London E15 4BQ
Mind*info*Line: 0845 766 0163
Website: www.mind.org.uk

Relatives and Residents Association
24 The Ivories
6–18 Northampton Street
London N1 2HY
Tel.: 020 7359 8148
Advice line: 020 7359 8136
Website: www.relres.org

Advises relatives and close friends of people in care homes on a range
of topics.

The Princess Royal Trust for Carers England
Unit 14, Bourne Court
Southend Road
Woodford Green
Essex IG8 8HD
Tel.: 0844 800 4361
Website: www.carers.org

The Princess Royal Trust for Carers Scotland
Charles Oakley House
125 West Regent Street
Glasgow G2 2SD
Tel.: 0141 221 5066

The Princess Royal Trust for Carers Wales
Victoria House
250 Cowbridge Road East
Canton
Cardiff CF5 1GZ
Tel.: 02920 221788

Relate
Premier House
Carolina Court
Lakeside
Doncaster DN4 5RA
Tel.: 0300 100 0234
Website: www.relate.org.uk

Offers relationship counselling and support. Call or visit website for local
branch details.

Samaritans
Chris
PO Box 9090
Stirling FK8 2SA
Tel.: 08457 909090
Website: www.samaritans.org

Further reading

Bayley, John, *Iris: A Memoir of Iris Murdoch*, Abacus, 2002

Brotchie, Jane, *Caring for Someone with Dementia*, Age Concern, 2003

Bryden, Christine, *Dancing with Dementia*, Jessica Kingsley, 2005

Buijssen, Huub, *The Simplicity of Dementia: A Guide for Family and Carers*, Jessica Kingsley, 2005

Burns, Prof. Alistair, *Your Guide to Alzheimer's Disease*, The Alzheimer's Society, 2005

Department of Health, *Living Well with Dementia: A National Dementia Strategy*, DH, 2009; also available at <www.dh.gov.uk>.

Goudge, Mary, *Choosing a Care Home*, How To Books, 2004

Hann, Lizi, *The Milk's in the Oven: A Booklet about Dementia for Children and Young People*, Mental Health Foundation, 2005

James, Oliver, *Contented Dementia: 24-hour Wraparound Care for Lifelong Well-being*, Vermillion, 2008

Kuhn, Daniel, *Alzheimer's Early Stages: First Steps for Family, Friends and Caregivers* (second edition), Hunter House, 2007

McCall, Bridget, *The Complete Carers' Guide*, Sheldon Press, 2007

Mace, Nancy and Rabins, Peter, *The 36-Hour Day: A Family Guide to Caring for Persons with Alzheimer's Disease, Related Dementing Illnesses and Memory Loss in Later Life* (revised edition), Grand Central Publishing, 2001

Smith, Dr Tom, *Living with Alzheimer's Disease*, Sheldon Press, 2005

Tugendhat, Julia, *Living with Grief and Loss*, Sheldon Press, 2005

Index

acupuncture 50
Admiral nurses 107
age as a risk factor in dementia 4
agent 79
aggression 38, 48–9
alcohol 7, 15, 69
aluminium 2–3
Alzheimer's Cafés 23
Alzheimer's disease 1–3
    drugs used to treat 41–3
    myths about 2–3
Alzheimer's Society 7, 23, 47, 105
anti-dementia drugs 41–4
antidepressants 47–8
appointee 79–80
Aricept 41
aromatherapy 49
assessment 81–3
    carer's 82
    community care 81–2, 87
attorney, lasting power of 18, 80

benefits 18, 77–9
bereavement 15, 104–5
bright light therapy 51–2

care homes
    choosing 90–2
    complaints about 93–4
    paying for 89
    settling in to 92–5
care plan 83
Care Quality Commission (CQC) 92
care, residential
    continuing relationship with
        relative in 94–5
    permanent 89–95
    temporary 87
carer
    coping with being 96–105
    finding the right 85–6
complaints 84
confusion 58
constipation 70–1

cost of care 84, 87
counselling 27, 46

dementia
    final stages of 104–5
    later stages of 100–2
    risk factors 4
denial 13–14
depression 44–8, 70
diagnosis
    family history of 5
    getting 11–12
    importance of 12–13
    reaction to 22–5
diet 7, 68
Down's syndrome 6
driving 21–2

eating 71–3
    see also weight loss, weight gain
Ebixa 43
Exelon 41
exercise 67–8
eyesight problems 70

family relationships 96–9
finances 18–19, 77–80
food see eating
forgetfulness 56–7
frontal lobe dementia 3
future, planning for the 17, 29, 33,
    96–7

gender as a risk factor 5
genetics 5
grief 98
guilt 103–4

hallucinations 11
health of carer 99–100
health problems in person with
    dementia 69–71
hearing problems 70
hiding things 62
holidays see respite care

identity
    jewellery 62
    loss of 23, 98
incontinence 73–6
inhibitions, loss of 63–4
intimacy 33–4, 40
    effect of dementia on 37–9

Korsakoff's syndrome 7

laundry 76
legal matters 18–20
Lewy body dementia 3, 11
life story book 53–4
living will 20

meals on wheels 80
medical history as a risk factor 6
memory
    aids to 81
    long-term 57
    loss of 55–6
memory box 54
mini Mental State Examination
    (MMSE) *see* testing
money *see* finances
music therapy 50–1

neurofibrillary tangles 2
night waking 60
nursing homes 87, 90

odd behaviour 58–65
odours 76

parent with dementia 26–9
partner of carer 98–9

partner with dementia 32–40
plaques 2, 6
practical help 80–1

relationship, changes in 24–5, 37
reminiscence therapy 52–3
Reminyl 41
repetitive behaviour 59–60
respite care 84–5, 87–8
restlessness 48, 60

sex
    increased interest in 35–6
    loss of interest in 35
    see also intimacy
sexual behaviour, difficult 36–7
sexuality 33–4
    while in residential care 39
shouting 64
siblings 29
sleep 60
smoking 8, 69
social services 72, 81, 83
social worker 79, 106
support groups 100
symptoms of dementia 8–9, 10, 11

testing 15–16
trailing 62

vascular dementia 3

wandering 60–2
weight gain 72–3
weight loss 72
will
    living 20
    making 19